The Romance of Old Annapolis Royal

THE HISTORICAL ASSOCIATION
OF ANNAPOLIS ROYAL

ROYAL EVER LOYAL

THE ROMANCE OF OLD
ANNAPOLIS
ROYAL

CHARLOTTE ISABELLA PERKINS

With an introduction by
Dr. Esmeralda Thornhill

BOULDER
PUBLICATIONS

Library and Archives Canada Cataloguing in Publication

Perkins, Charlotte Isabella, 1878-1964
   The romance of old Annapolis Royal / Charlotte Isabella Perkins.

Previous ed.: Annapolis Royal, N.S. : Historical Association of Annapolis
   Royal, 1988.
ISBN 978-1-927099-11-7

   1. Annapolis Royal (N.S.)--History. I. Title.

FC2349.A55Z57 2012   971.6'33   C2012-902326-4

Boulder Publications edition, copyright 2012
With permission of the Historical Association of Annapolis Royal
www.boulderpublications.ca

Editor: Vanessa MacKinnon
Cover design and layout: Erica Allanach

Front cover images: Nova Scotia Archives
"Port Royal", photostatic copy of map originally published in Les Voyages du
   Sieur de Champlain (1613); NSA Map Collection: F/239 - 1609 -
   Annapolis Royal.
"Barracks, Fort Anne, Annapolis Royal, NS", W.R. MacAskill, photographer;
   NSA, W.R. MacAskill fonds, 1987-453 no. 4624.

Printed in Canada

We acknowledge financial support of the Government of Newfoundland and
Labrador for our publishing program through the Department of Tourism,
Culture and Recreation.

We acknowledge financial support for our publishing program by the
Government of Canada and the Department of Canadian Heritage through the
Canada Book Fund.

TABLE OF CONTENTS

SPECIAL INTRODUCTION

Although The Romance of Old Annapolis Royal was originally published in 1924, the current reissue attests to the publication's value as a useful and popular chronicle depicting town life in Nova Scotia's Annapolis Royal. With the inclusion of this Special Introduction, this 2012 republishing opens the curtain on important factors that contextualize, clarify, and complement the book's contents.

In the nearly nine decades since the recorded small-town "slices of life" and moments in time were captured, freeze-framed, and published, times have changed, and so too the legal, demographic, and social landscapes. The 1982 adoption of a new Constitution with an entrenched Charter of Human Rights and Freedoms has contributed immeasurably to Canada's ongoing evolution into a "just society" where equality is predicated on the bedrock principles of non-discrimination and the intrinsic worth and dignity of each and every human being. A flattering self-portrait of our country as a welcoming "Open Door" haven and democratic model of political equality regularly shields us from criticism at home and abroad. But to what extent is this not an overly touted myth? For with increasing frequency, multiracial and multicultural realities are relentlessly compelling new "reality checks"—pressing us to ask critical questions that interrogate our national history and challenge the conventionally accepted conduct and discourse of our nation-state. This is particularly applicable to our dealings with African-descended and Aboriginal peoples.

This Introduction constitutes one such reality check. It arises out of a desire to sensitize readers to the dangers of uncritically accepting works or descriptions of Blacks and Aboriginals penned by others, especially by those whose moorings and perceptions remain mired in the ignoble principles and practices of colonialism.

The Romance of Old Annapolis Royal contains references and allusions to Black and Aboriginal peoples, information of a past period that has been and is rightly deemed to be of historical value. But, far from evoking "romance," many of these references, so imbued with the trope of 'race,' amount to disparaging, derogatory, dismissive labels that misrepresent Black reality and continue to feed tenacious stereotypes. Down through the years these stereotypes have persisted and still stubbornly persist in defying correction; they are not national heirlooms to be treasured, preserved, and passed on from generation to generation. Such epistemological violence must end.

This Introduction is an attempt to strike a much-needed balance. While acknowledging the historical value of dated information, it aims to provide, from a critical anti-racist stance, a 'race' lens or filter through which readers will realize that un-interrogated data, or language that is overtly or covertly racist, both contribute to reinforcing, renewing, and re-inscribing racism and racial discrimination. These dynamics of oppression effectively transport the racism of the past into the present, shoring up and perpetuating racism's legacy of violence and inequality.

Boulder Publications is to be commended for its insight, foresight, and courage to grapple with this ethical dilemma. The appeal and concerns fuelling the request to contextualize this sixth republishing resonate with my own long-standing study and critical analysis. To a great degree, Aboriginals and peoples of African descent have been marginalized, shut out of society and rendered invisible. Like pages of History gone missing, our respective authentic histories—in our own voices—have been marginalized, omitted from the national narrative and the "material reality" of our lives erased from cognition.

These "missing pages" of Black and Aboriginal history are all too often replaced by a White-onlooker gaze or view that treats racialized individuals and communities as passive objects rather than as subjects in the drama of nation-building. Furthermore, tantamount to derision, this onlooker treatment minimizes and obfuscates or obscures the hideous and cruel material reality of bondage experienced by its victim-survivors. In addressing a small sector of the missing pages of Canadian history, this initiative also targets the marginalization and erasure of Aboriginal and African-descended peoples that dismiss our contributions to the history and development of Canada.

It was an honour for me to accept this challenge because it essentially spoke to my averred mission statement as the first scholar to inaugurate the James Robinson Johnston Endowed Chair in Black Canadian Studies, namely, "to bring Black culture, reality, perspective, experiences and concerns into the Academy." In essence, this Introduction constitutes an affirmation: of those unknown and unmentioned legions of Aboriginals displaced, dislocated, dispossessed of their land, and scattered by forces beyond their control; of the multitudes of unknown and unnamed Blacks who toiled in the fields, kitchens, laundries, railroads, mines, sweatshops, and factories not of their choosing.

It is a validation of all their yearnings and determination for dignity—an homage to their small acts of resistance which can, will, and are turning into a social force for Justice.

While this Introduction cannot undo the perceptions of the past, I hope, however, that it will awaken and foster in readers an abiding desire to probe and examine critically records already established, as well as those in production.

Dr. Esmeralda M.A. Thornhill
Professor of Law
First James Robinson Johnston Endowed Chair
in Black Canadian Studies (1996 – 2002)

Halifax, Nova Scotia

THE ROMANCE OF OLD ANNAPOLIS
ANNAPOLIS ROYAL, NOVA SCOTIA

Former pamphlets of mine, containing historical facts and stories, having been favourably received, I have decided to reprint them with additions and revisions under the title of *The Romance of Old Annapolis Royal*, all of which is affectionately dedicated to my native town, Annapolis Royal.

— Charlotte Isabella Perkins, A.D. 1934

Revised by the writer, 1912, and republished by the Historical Association of Annapolis Royal, Nova Scotia, Canada, with permission.

PORT ROYAL

About this ancient earth work and this wall,
Where rude-spiked gates on heavy hinges hung,
The shouts of armies many a time have rung,
And thundering cannon sounded loud o'er all,
Here night and morn the echoing bugles call
Close to the fartherest wooded hill-tops clung;
Here, with her lilies to the breezes flung,
France held Arcadia in romantic thrall.
Here, Bourbon nobles earned the fleur-de-lis,
And waved the white flag of the Bourbon Kings,
Here Acadie's first convert, Membertou,
The aged Micmac chieftain bent the knee
To Christ; and here on wide expanded wings
The hostile fleets of British sovereigns flew.

— Dr. Arthur H. W. Eaton

A BRIEF BIT OF ITS HISTORY

Block House
(From an 1884 photo)

"There are few localities in America around which the memories of the shadowy past cluster more interestingly than around the ancient town of Annapolis Royal."

— *Bridgetown Free Press*, 1865

Our romance begins in the spring of 1604, the year in which Sieur de Monts was granted a charter from King Henry IV to Christianize and colonize all that country then called L'Acadie. With him a gay motley crowd of priests, noblemen, and peasants, 120 in all, set sail from

France in four ships, Samuel de Champlain being geographer. After visiting several places along the coast, they came to what is now Annapolis Basin. So pleased were they with the beautiful panorama of land and water that opened out before them that Champlain immediately gave it the name of Port Royal or Royal Harbour. He wrote of it: "We entered one of the most beautiful ports which I had seen on these coasts where two thousand vessels could anchor in safety." When Lescarbot came, he wrote: "It was a thing so marvellous to see, the fair distances and the largeness of it — I wondered how so fair a place did remain desert."

In 1605 they came back and then began the "first durable settlement" in all that country north of St. Augustine. At Port Royal now stands a replica of the Habitation of the French, reproduced faithfully due to the vision and efforts of the late Mrs. Harriet Tabor Richardson of Cambridge, Massachusetts, USA, and Annapolis Royal and Port Royal Associates.

The initiative was recognized by the Canadian government and the work completed by the Dominion government. It now is maintained as a National Historic Park and attracts hundreds of visitors yearly.

It was in this vicinity that the first wheat was grown, the first Canadian vessel built, the first road making undertaken. Farther up the river the first mill was erected, and where the existing fort of Annapolis Royal now stands, the first farming was carried on. In this area, too, originated the apple-growing industry of Nova Scotia.

In that early wilderness life, all the historians tell the captivating story of Champlain's first social Order — "L'Ordre de Bon Temps"[1] in the winter of 1606-1607.

We can, in imagination, picture the scene: the low-ceilinged room; its roaring fireplace; the long table with its steaming viands; the jovial countenances of the Frenchmen as they drank each other's health; the savages who squatted about. Around that truly festive board were Champlain, Baron de Poutrincourt, Biencourt his son, Lescarbot, Louis Hebert, Daniel Hays, and other makers of history.

Lescarbot adds: "And whatever our gourmands at home may think, we found as good cheer at Port Royal as they in Paris and at a cheaper rate."

As guests at these functions were always the sagamore Membertou, who claimed equal rights with the Frenchmen by virtue of his rank, and 20 to 30 savages. This centenarian has been called "the most redoubtable savage that ever lived in the history of man."

Near Port Royal, as chief of a palisaded village, he had mustered some 400 warriors. Parkman says: "In deeds of blood and treachery he had no rival in the Acadian forests. In behalf of this martial concourse, he had proved himself a sturdy beggar pursuing Poutrincourt with daily petitions, now for a bushel of beans, now for a basket of bread, now for a barrel of wine to regale his greasy crew." History repeats itself; in 1930 the chief of the Mi'kmaq Indians, Benjamin

---

[1] There is still "The Order of Good Cheer," as we say it in English, as a community club in the town. In the year 1934, partly under the auspices of this Order, with Rev. Leo Murphy as promoter, a grand Indian carnival was successfully staged. It will long be remembered as one of the finest events in our social history.

Pictou, celebrated his 100th birthday when he held a large "At Home" at his residence in Lequille near the town.

Another scene in that early life was the enacting of a play or masque, "Theatre de Neptune," with the unique distinction of being performed on the water in canoes by both Indians and Frenchmen. It was written by that versatile genius Lescarbot to set forth "some piece of merriment" on the return of Poutrincourt in 1606, for whom the fort was decorated in laurel. A tablet placed in the Museum in 1926 commemorates the "Birth of the Drama in North America at Port Royal, in 1606."

The bright happy prospects of the new settlement soon came to an end. In 1613, Captain Samuel Argall, of Jamestown, Virginia, completely destroyed the fort and all marks of French power with the exception of the mill farther up the river. England now claimed the country. Under King James I of England and Scotland, Sir William Alexander received a charter in 1621 for the promoting of colonization in Nova Scotia. Later, the Order of Knights Baronets of Nova Scotia was created to further this scheme. With the arrival of Sir William here in 1629 with 70 Scotch colonists, the fort became known as Charles Fort. Only fragmentary accounts are written of that colony which began so brilliantly and ended so tragically. But from that ill-fated company we received our name, Nova Scotia; also under Charles I, 1625, our flag — the only province until recently having a flag of its own — and our coat of arms, perhaps the finest from the heraldic standpoint.

The 300th anniversary of this event was marked by a Scottish festival, held on the fort grounds in Annapolis Royal in 1929. An attractive two days' programme of things Scottish was well carried out.

After 1629, for a century and a quarter, there ensued a long and bitter struggle for the possession of the country. Little Port Royal, the stronghold and key to all Acadia, became, as one writer expresses it, "the football of the nations." Seven times it changed hands between the French and English, and 14 times the fort was besieged by French, English, or Indians. With its final capture in 1710, it became a British possession. Subercase, the French governor, capitulated to General Nicholson of Massachusetts with five New England regiments and a regiment of Royal Marines, the last having been commissioned and armed by Queen Anne at her own expense. The brave Subercase with his 150 men, "all in a miserable condition," marched out with all the honours of war. The British troops marched in with drums beating and flags flying, hoisted the Union Jack, and drank the Queen's health. Thus French Port Royal became the English Annapolis Royal in honour of the then reigning Queen Anne. Haliburton says: "The expense incurred by New England in the conquest amounted to £23,000, afterwards reimbursed by Parliament." The key of the citadel of Port Royal was handed over to Nicholson, who took it to Boston, where in time it came into the custody of the Massachusetts Historical Society. It took three men to bring it back here, not by strength — though it is large — but by the courtesy of that Society.

Even after the conquest, it was a long time before peace finally settled over Annapolis Royal. There were attacks and rumours of attacks, all of which retarded its growth. The prestige which Port Royal had enjoyed as the capital of the province ceased when Halifax was founded in 1749. The few remaining soldiers of the garrison here were removed to Fredericton, New Brunswick, in 1854.

In 1932, "I.C.R." wrote in the *Halifax Herald*, quoted from the *Free Press* just as it appeared in 1818:

"Annapolis Royal, 5th June, 1818. Yesterday being the anniversary of His Majesty's Birthday, a royal salute and feu de joie was fired in honour of the day. Immediately after a grand levee was held at the Commandant's, at which all the respectables attended. The amusements of the day concluded by a most splendid ball at the Garrison Mess Room, which was brilliantly and numerously attended and which, for beauty and fashion, was never equalled. The utmost cordiality prevailed and the company did not separate till an early hour the next morning. We are extremely sorry to hear that a report prevails that it is His Lordship's intention to remove the detachment 60th, stationed at this post; a circumstance much to be regretted, owing to the uniformly good conduct of the men and the high esteem in which the officers are held by this old and respected city, between whom the greatest harmony has ever existed."

That was the beginning of the end of Annapolis Royal as a garrison city. A few weeks later the same paper reported the arrival at Halifax from Annapolis Royal of a troop ship. And that's how Halifax became a big city and Annapolis Royal a small town.

The expulsion of the Acadians (1755) has been made memorable the world over in Longfellow's "Evangeline." At Annapolis Royal about 1,600 were placed on vessels. Some escaped to the woods and afterwards made their way back, but very few of their descendants are here.

The last outstanding historic event was the coming of the Loyalists. For many years previous to the American Revolution there had been a steady immigration to

Annapolis Royal and vicinity from the United States, but in 1783 2,500 were added to the population. The Rev. Jacob Bailey, himself a Loyalist, reported that the church, courthouse, and stores were crowded and that "hundreds of people of education and refinement have no shelter whatever." From that company we received the DeLanceys from New York — our most distinguished family — and many others of note, including Major Grant's family, one of whose daughters became the mother of Judge Thomas C. Haliburton.

Murdock says: "In 1720 the trade of Annapolis Royal was carried on by four or five sloops from Boston which commonly made three voyages in the season, bringing some woollen manufactures of Great Britain but mostly West Indian products. These they exchanged for furs and feathers to the value of £10,000 yearly without paying duties outward or inward."

Walking along the pretty, peaceful streets of Annapolis Royal today, one sees little to remind him of its stormy past. The fort that had been so often besieged and so often changed masters, no longer echoes to the signal gun or the sentry's "All's well." The present fort, the third and last built by the French, is now maintained as Fort Anne National Historic Park by the Canadian government and attracts thousands of visitors yearly (over 18,000 in 1951). The buildings of the French regime have largely disappeared, but the powder magazine, built by Subercase in 1708 of Caen limestone brought from France, still defies the ravages of time. It would seem to stand as his own memorial.[2] The Officers Quarters built under the direction of the Duke of Kent in 1797 (the cornerstone can still be seen) was estab-

---

[2] A memorial tablet to Daniel Auger de Subercase was unveiled in 1932.

lished as a museum through the efforts of Mr. L. M. Fortier, the first Honorary Superintendent of Fort Anne National Park. It houses many relics of the historic past, but some of its antique features had to be sacrificed to render it fireproof.

The happiest and biggest event in the town's later history was the celebration of its 300th anniversary, June, 1904. Representatives from the British, French, and American nations gathered in the old fort to do honour to the memory of those illustrious pioneers — de Monts, Champlain and their brave comrades. The culmination of this tercentenary was the laying of the cornerstone of the de Monts monument. Once again the flag of France flew over these old ramparts, side by side with those of America and Britain. It was a time of peace and goodwill between nations.

> Faut-il abandonner les beautés de ce lieu
> Et dire à Port Royal un éternal adieu?
> — Lescarbot

Sally Port and Officers' Quarters

Beyond local histories, those wishing to delve deeper will find it "writ large" in the works of Champlain, Lescarbot, Haliburton, Murdock, Campbell, and Calnek and Savary.

OLD HOUSES

There is a mystery old houses know
The years will ever keep inviolate;
An essence of the past, the long ago
That hovers round the eaves, the muted gate,
The shaded gravelwalk that idly winds
Between the ranks of tulips time has sundered;
There is a secret guarded by shut blinds,
The bold and prying world has never plundered.

If you have loved old houses, never yearn
To break their seals of silence and of death;
It is enough forgotten dreams return
Within the lilac's faint and fitful breath.
Pause at the gate and feel your heart expand,
But never hope to know, or understand.

— Anderson M. Scruggs

CONCERNING OLD HOUSES
ALONG ST. GEORGE STREET

Not far away we saw the port,
The strange old-fashioned silent town,
The lighthouse, the dismantled fort,
The wooden houses quaint and brown.

— LongfeIIow

These are reminiscences and anecdotes concerning the old houses of Annapolis Royal, most of which range in age from 100 years to more. Few remain as they were originally, some having been destroyed by fire, others have been modernized, and still others torn down. They were for the most part small wooden buildings, certainly not pretentious, while low sloping roofs, dormer windows, and centre doors characterized the predominating type. Set in gardens of old-fashioned flowers, with the main paths leading from whitewashed paling fences, there was a charm about them that was very real. But when we think of the other side of the picture, say in wintertime, with none of the modern conveniences, the rooms large, no furnaces — not even cooking stoves in the early days — we would find no comfort in them today.

Governor Paul Mascarene gives us an interesting description of his home here in 1740. "My apartment," he writes his daughter Margaret, "contains four rooms, all contiguous to one another, the first something larger than our fore room (in Boston), the floor none of the best, is covered with painted cloth. The white walls are hung in part with four large Pictures of Mr. Smibert — a walnutt chest of drawers,

23

a mahogany table, and six pretty good chairs fill, in some measure, the remainder. Over the mantel piece are a dozen of arms kept clean and in good order, with other warlike accoutrements. In this Room, I dine sometimes alone but often with one or more of my friends. A door opens from this into my bed-room where my field bed, four chairs, the little round table, a desk to write upon, and my clothes chest are all the furniture that adorns it. The two closets on the side of the chimney serve, the one to keep my papers, the other to hang my clothes. In the great room one of the closets dispos'd on the side of the chimney is made to keep my drinkables for daily use, my case of bottles and such like. The other is for a kind of pantry and at the same time for a passage to another room wherein I keep my meal, flour, fresh and salt provisions. This communicates by a door to my kitchen and is the way by which I go every morning to order my dinner and give out what provision is necessary for it. The other communication from the kitchen to the great room is by the parade as far as from our back kitchen to our back door. I have a bell to call my servant both from my dining and bed rooms. My Domesticks are a good old honest soldyer who makes my bed, keeps my clothes and my apartment clean and attends me very diligently and faithfully, another who was my cook when your sister (Betty) was here attends me in the same office, they have a boy to assist them both. All three discharge their tasks in an easy and quiet manner and give little or no trouble. The morning, now especially in winter time, I generally pass att home in usefull and diverting employments. I sometimes dine abroad. The afternoons I visit some of the families in our fort town, and the evenings, Capn. Handfield, Lt. Amherst and three or four more of our officers meet att one another's houses over a game of ombre for half pence, and part att nine, when after an hour enjoy'd quietly in my own room I go to bed. These rounds I have done for these months."

Follow with me along St. George Street, that street which has witnessed many stirring times and where now peace and beauty reign. Beginning in Lower Town, and oldest part, there lived men who have left their social and intellectual influence, both in town and province. Some of them were Andrew Ritchie, MPP, of Scotland, a brother of Judge Thomas Ritchie; Henkells, Snedens, Robertsons, LeCains (Lequesne), Lovetts, Davoues, Jameses, Haliburtons, and Roaches (their house still standing, built in 1810). Colonel DeLancey, Loyalist of 1783, also lived in this part of the town for a while. The house this family probably occupied was a sturdy one built in the days of the French. It had heavy timbers with double rows of studdings and filled with brick — considered strong enough to withstand a siege. It was sold to the Roman Catholic Church and torn down in 1870.

The residence of Mrs. Griffin O'Dell today was built more than 80 years ago by Mr. Corey O'Dell of Saint John, New Brunswick. A large substantial house of Victorian architecture, it contains 14 rooms and a shop. Here Mr. O'Dell had a general merchandise business, favoured by a good stand opposite the ferry. This house has never been changed, and the O'Dells have always been the occupants.

Mr. Wm. Quigley's bungalow now stands on the site that once accommodated the hotel known as the Commercial House. The hotel stood opposite the old ferry slip and was built by John Hall, who came to Annapolis Royal in 1760. Mr. Hall carried on a large mercantile business, and ships were built and launched right across the street. In the old coaching days it was one of the stopping places for the picturesque covered coach and four, or tally-ho, as it drove in from Halifax. On entering the town the driver blew his bugle, which was the signal for the townspeople to flock out to greet the travellers and to get the news from the outside world. Belcher's Almanac, 1833, gives the distance as 130 miles, fare being £2, with three trips a week.

Bailey House

Pre-eminent amongst all the houses in that part of the town is the old landmark, the Bailey house, built 170 years ago by Colonel Wm. Robertson, MPP, and corner-wise, so it is said, to spite his neighbour from looking up the street; however, we can hardly credit that, knowing the reputation of the man. It is credited yet with being "solid as a rock" and having carpentry of the best. Colonel Robertson's son James, who married Charlotte Williams, and was the grandfather of the Robertson of Manchester, Robertson & Allison, Saint

John, sold it to the Baileys, that is, Thomas Bailey (son of the Rev. Jacob) for £300. He was appointed barrack master in 1808 in the fort, and when he died, his wife and three daughters kept it for many years as an aristocratic boarding house for officers, clergy, and professional men who came to town. "Sam Slick" was a frequenter here. He it was who gave it the name of "Marm Bailey's," but his Annapolis Royal story "The Snow Wreath" was not written in that house but in another farther up the street, on one of those nights when Mrs. Bailey's was taxed to capacity. The Duke of Kent danced at a ball in this house when visiting Annapolis Royal in 1794.

Marm Bailey was a large handsome woman; she was also capable and kept a first-class establishment. She excelled in the culinary department — her moose muffle soup being exported to England. It may be of interest to housekeepers today to learn of the ingredients used in its making: after preparation of the muffle, knuckle of veal, onions, thyme, marjoram, clove, cayenne, salt, force-meat balls fried in butter, tomato catsup, and yolks of 12 hard-boiled eggs were added, and lastly a bottle of old port. This, like all other cooking, was done on a fireplace which took cordwood stick lengths. Long after the garrison was removed, officers came here to go moose hunting in the depth of winter; there was no closed season.

The Misses Bailey (three) did fine sewing, such as the making of trousseaux and altar linen, at which they were adept. An excerpt from a book of their time reads: "There are in town a number of inns, and summer guests are also made welcome and comfortable in many of the private residences: in one of the latter, a large old-fashioned house with antique furniture, three sisters reside who possess the quaint dignity and manner of the old school and here one would feel as if visiting at one's grandfather's and be made pleasantly at home." Another reads: "On the visit of the Marquis of Lorne in 1880, after seeing the objects of interest in and around the town, he expressed a wish to call upon Mrs. Elizabeth Bailey, one of the most aged persons in this County and who, he had been informed, had been introduced to the Duke of Kent during his stay in Annapolis Royal. He thoroughly enjoyed the conversation with this aged matron as she told of the interesting reminiscences of the Royal Duke and of the reference to Charles Percy Bailey, her husband's brother, a young man of prepossessing appearance and of much intellectual promise. His R.H. [Royal Highness] was so pleased that he gave him a commission in his own regiment in which he rose to the rank of Captain."

Naturally, these young ladies came in the way of meeting many admirers, of whom Sam Slick was one. Miss Sarah used to take pleasure in telling how she would have none of his attentions as her heart had been given to one Captain C. Bell, who had died in France while there for his health. We do not believe it was from spitefulness that he dubbed her "Corporal Prim" but rather because of the grey and red checked linsey dress, buttoned straight up and down, front and back, which she then wore. Sarah also liked to speak of another admirer, an officer, who one day went to call, but finding her out, said he would know how to find her. The ground being covered with new fallen snow, he traced her steps as far as the Grassies (The Gables) from her footprints — there being no others so dainty.

The late Dr. Robinson remembers Judge Haliburton taking the *Maid of the Mist*, the boat that plied between here and Saint John and docked opposite the Bailey house. Being late, it waited for him with old Rose Fortune (coloured), the notorious "baggage smasher," going ahead and beckoning, "Come along, Jedge, come along," and he handing her an English shilling — a big tip in those days — saying "goodbye, my black Venus." It was Rose's pride to black the boots for all the gentlemen who went there. Father Butler, passing her on the street one day, heard her saying to herself, "He looks well and his boots look well."

Here are copies of two letters which have been preserved — one from Lady Mulgrave:

Mrs. Bailey:

I am quite sorry to have forgotten acknowledging the receipt of the worsted socks before, but I mislaid your daughter's letter and only found it last eve. Lord Mulgrave was quite delighted with his socks and says if you can remember the size you may make him another dozen pairs as soon as you like. Lord Althrop's fitted him beautifully.

Am glad you have begun the quilt but don't tire your eyes over it as the colour is trying.

Your sincere well wisher,

Laura Mulgrave.
Government House, Halifax,
October 6th, 1859.

Another from Bishop J. Inglis:

> Halifax, March 1st.
>
> My dear Mrs. Bailey:
>
> Captain and Mrs. Williams who are friends of ours purpose to leave here on Tuesday next for Windsor from whence they will proceed by the coach and arrive at Annapolis on Friday evening. They will have two children and two maid servants and should the weather be unfavourable they may be detained on the road as the conveyance at present is only by an open wagon. I have promised them that you will have warm rooms for them and every comfort Annapolis can supply and you will oblige us by making them your special charge! etc., etc.
>
> John, Nova Scotia.
>
> Captain Williams will remain with you till the steamer goes to Saint John.

Rev. Jacob Bailey says: "The best house in Annapolis with two acres of garden costs me £20."

When Mrs. Bailey died, the daughters declared there was a halo about her head. They were left with very little means. In those days there were no social services, no old age pensions, and the like, so they would have fared badly but for the kindness of friends and the proceeds of the sale of a piece of furniture now and again. Miss Sarah, the last surviving member of her family, went to live at the rectory and gave the house to Saint Luke's Church. Rented as a tenement, it soon became dilapidated in appearance and was looked upon rather derisively as "only the old Bailey House." Miss Suzanne Haliburton, since acquiring it as a residence, has done valiant work in restoring something of its original graciousness.

Next in order is the old McNamara house — so named from the schoolteacher who had a high school in Rev. Bailey's time. Some of us remember old Mrs. McNamara, a pathetic figure in the decline of life, gathering bouquets of "bleeding heart," "ragged robin," and "old man," etc. from her garden and selling them for a pittance to buy gin. The house, then a quaint picturesque one, but now completely changed since it was damaged by fire, was also the home of Captain John Robertson, a prosperous merchant who, like his brother James, did a large West Indian business. Here he bought his bride, Bathiah Davoue, at the age of 17, and at their wedding reception received the guests seated upon a throne. Captain John, familiarly called "Commodore" or "Port Admiral Robertson," was of good descent and, through his eccentricities and wit, a "character" in the town. The story of the family name is a pretty incident of Scotch history. The Robertsons, who were originally Clan Dounachaidh or Sons of Duncan, came to the aid of Robert Bruce at the Battle of Bannockburn and rendered him signal service. When the battle was over, the King rode up to Clan Dounachaidh and addressing them said, "Hitherto ye have been called the sons of Duncan but henceforth ye shall be called my children, that is, the Sons of Robert."

Then follow several other houses, closely set, leading up to Church Street. They used to have fenced-in gardens in front which took in most of the sidewalk, but the street commissioners were not particular about well-defined property lines at that time. Where the Post Office now stands is said to be the site of Colonel Vetch's home; it was Colonel Vetch who took such an active part in the conquest of Port Royal and was its first British governor.

Near here, too, the Widow Cooper lived in a large white house. In one of the regiments stationed here was an officer named Captain Gee. He had run through his pay and was anxious to get back to England, but he lacked the funds. Now, Mrs. Cooper was a charming widow and rich. She could easily supply any travelling expenses, so he persuaded her to elope with him. After travelling a while in Scotland and England, she paying the bills, he deserted her. In a beautifully written letter (1812), Mrs. Cooper, who was then in Hull, England, wrote home to Mrs. Bailey of the wonderful vista the lights of that city made and how hard it would be to go to the dark streets of Annapolis, and that she would as soon think of going to "John O'Groats" as returning.

But that she did return is evident from the following story, which is told as true: When on her deathbed, Mrs. Williams and her daughter Anna went to sit with her, and in the night Mrs. Cooper asked for a drink of water. Mrs. Williams was about to get it when a Negress, wearing a turban and rings in her ears, glided into the room carrying a glass of water on a tray. Going to the bed she gave the water to Mrs. Cooper and then disappeared. Miss Anna was so frightened she hid herself in her mother's arms, saying, "Oh, mother, what was that?" Mrs. Williams, to calm her daughter, said, "I don't think it was anything." She then went out to where there was a pitcher of water and a glass. Pouring out a glassful, she brought it to Mrs. Cooper, saying, "I have brought you a glass of water." Whereupon Mrs. Cooper thanked her and said, "I don't care for any for (calling by name her old slave she had owned years ago) has just brought me a delicious glass of water."

It is also clear that Mrs. Cooper returned to Annapolis Royal from the epitaph appearing in the old cemetery, which reads as follows:

Sacred
to the memory of
MRS. HENRIETTA COOPER
who departed this life
March 24, 1854
Aged 83 years
Blessed are the dead that lie in the Lord.

Mrs. Cooper owned all the property between that of Mr. John Harris and that of Mrs. Warren Harris — 22 acres in all. It was rented for £1 a year or given over to the poor to plant.

There stood next to the Post Office the Bonavista Hotel — a fine building of three stories with a drugstore in the exact spot where the Cornwallis Pharmacy is today. When Mrs. Maud Malcolm lived there with her mother, Mrs. Willett, it was the scene of a tragedy. A widowed lady, Mrs. Dakin, who boarded with them, kept a lending library and a novelty shop and, perhaps could be added, a little gossip shop too, for it was a handy place for people to "drop in." One lovely moonlit winter's night Mrs. Dakin, known to be of a romantic temperament, is presumed to have ventured out to where the snow and ice cakes were piled on the wharf opposite for the purpose of looking at the moonlit scene. It seems she either fell or slipped on an ice cake and was carried downstream. She had left the lamp burning in her room and everything else in order as though life was to go on as usual. When she failed to return home, friends searched and inquired all over town, to no avail. Nothing more was heard of her until the spring, when a fisherman near Digby spied a dark object. It was the decapitated body of a woman, dressed in black and having on a cameo brooch. The cameo later proved the identity of Mrs. Dakin.

Where the Capitol Theatre now stands (formerly King's Theatre) lived Henry Goldsmith, lawyer and collector of His Majesty's Customs. Later John Whitman acquired the property, and his family of six sons and three daughters, for the most part, became influential and wealthy in distant parts.

The David Bonnett house, where the Bank of Nova Scotia is now located, later belonged to the Corbitts for generations. Not having enough wharfage protection, the ice cakes would beat against the house along this part, so that in the spring it would be necessary to put in new underpinning. That reminds us of the great Saxby gale (1869), when a boat rode right through the lower part of the street.

Opposite the Bank of Nova Scotia is the late Mr. A. M. King's house, which was built by John Adams about 1712. It was of a pretty type of Colonial architecture containing a store, having trees and garden in front, but now incorporated as the large building we see today. It was the birthplace of Judge Thomas Ritchie.

The present brick shop of Mr. Charles Bower, now a place of business for heating and plumbing, saw in the past a very different atmosphere. It was built by the McLaughlin Bros. of England and named London House. They ran a first-class establishment offering dry goods, rich silks, satins, carpets, and millinery, etc., making yearly buying trips to England.

No one seems to know the beginning of the Annapolis Royal Hotel, but in making alterations in recent years a coin bearing the date of 1749 was found, which may be some clue to its age. More than 100 years ago, Mrs. Sinclair gave turkey suppers to the Annapolis Royal sports of that time in this house, which was known as Frederick Sinclair's Inn.

The first Masonic Lodge meeting in Canada was held here in 1738 by Major Erasmus James Phillips in what Colonel Frederick Sinclair used to call his "large room below stairs," and it is said that "it was a great convenience for the Craft to pass from labour to refreshment," which latter was indulged in frequently enough. We read that in 1791 this room was offered for the purpose of holding Supreme and Inferior Courts and Sessions. The many different owners have each had a hand in making alterations. Modern doors and windows have been substituted, extensions on the sides and back added, so that now it has lost all signs of antiquity. The house faced a hay slip on the opposite side and from this ran a road connecting with St. James Street. It is to be regretted that this building was not taken over early in its history and retained as a Masonic shrine. As it stands now, it is "unhonoured and unsung." The stagecoach used to stop at the side door, where the passengers would alight and the coach proceed to the stable beyond.

Then follows the apartment house of Mr. J. Gesner, built 100 years ago by Mr. Antonio Gavaza as a residence for his family. It was furnished as well as the period afforded. The front has been made over and it is the last of the Colonial type left, although there were several in the town.

Lieutenant Hudson, of the 60th Rifles, lived in the next house and opposite was the Gray House, so-called for its colour and the name of the people living there. Mr. Gray came to Annapolis Royal in 1842 and descendants of his in the Cunningham family still own the property. Mr. Gray was in his time an authority on the history of Port Royal. Dr. C. B. Cunningham, druggist and dentist, was an ardent promoter concerning the town's welfare.

The Williams house, made famous from its being the birthplace of Sir Fenwick Williams, was one of the oldest and best dwellings in the village. It stood where the Royal Bank now is and was removed in 1874. One part of it was moved to a position opposite the present skating rink and has been renovated. It was typical of the substantially built houses of that time: its walls set with clay and rushes a foot in thickness, and having an enormous centre chimney and large fireplaces. The interior was finished in pine, dark brown boards that shone like glass. The same material panelled the narrow crooked stairway, sheathed the walls, and covered the floors, these last having boards 18 inches wide and 1½ inches thick. In the front rooms were hand-carved mouldings with deep seats disposed on either side of the windows.

Mrs. Owen tells the story of Sir Fenwick's three sisters: "When they wished to make a smart appearance at the balls that were held, usually in the Assembly Hall near the Garrison gate, they were forced to use both wits and fingers as their purse was a short one, sometimes manufacturing their own shoes and gloves. On one occasion, when their father had forbidden their going to a certain ball, he came in unexpectedly and found them in anticipation of the event, dyeing their dresses over the fire." At this he threw a bucket of water over dresses and fire ruining at one and the same time finery and fire. The handsome crimson brocade dress of Mrs. Williams was remembered for years, as it was afterwards cut up for hangings for St. Luke's Church.

When Sir Fenwick returned to his native town as hero of Kars (Crimean War), Annapolis was in fete for the occasion. Arriving by steamer at the ferry slip, he was met by volunteers who formed in procession. Mounted on a fine black charger, which became frightened at the callathumpians, he was obliged to retire. At the Court House Square, where cannon were mounted, he received everybody, and how proud they must have been to claim him as their own, both hero and friend. On blockhouse hill in the fort, the lanterns when lighted were so ingeniously arranged as to form the word KARS, and from every window small tallow candles added to the display — this latter a way of celebrating at such a time.

General Williams House

General Williams never married. It is said a romance in early youth connected with Madame Winniett was the primary cause of his remaining a bachelor. When he visited his home, he never failed to call on his admired friend. Throughout his entire life he showed an interest in her by many acts of "substantial though delicate kindnesses."

Two of the swords which had been presented to Sir Fenwick for valour were shown at a meeting of the Annapolis Royal Historical Association. In writing about these swords he said: "Of all the proofs which I have or shall receive of this too general sentiment in my favour the sword voted to me by Nova Scotia is the most acceptable to my heart, and when I again come within sight of the shores of that land where I first drew breath, I shall feel that I am one hundred times requited for all that I have gone through during the eventful years of the last terrible struggle." The Queen conferred a baronetcy and Parliament voted a pension of £100 sterling on him. In the Chateau de Ramezay, Montreal, is shown a jewelled casket, a gift of His Royal Highness the Duke of Kent to Mrs. Williams, mother of Sir Fenwick.

A tablet now on the Royal Bank, which was unveiled by the Duke of Connaught during his term as Governor General, reads:

THIS TABLET
marks the site of the birthplace of
GENERAL SIR WILLIAM FENWICK WILLIAMS, BARONET
1799-1883
"The Hero of Kars"
Pasha of Turkey
Grand Officer Legion of Honour, France

Member of the British Parliament
Commander-in-Chief Forces British North America
Governor of Gibraltar
Constable of the Tower
Lt. Governor of his native Province

NOVA SCOTIA HISTORICAL SOCIETY

The story about this house is as follows: When Miss Tobias and Miss Leslie, young ladies of the town, used to go out riding in the morning, they were not allowed to go unaccompanied, so a young man, George Ince (afterwards Colonel Ince), made an appointment to go with them, which he did not fulfill. The following evening he went to see these young ladies and they chaffed him about having overslept. "No," he said. "If you had seen what I saw last night you would have not felt like turning out in the morning." Full of curiosity they asked, "Why, George, what did you see?" Then he related how he was asleep in the east bedroom of the Williams house when, in the middle of the night, he awoke, startled, to see a soldier glide into the room, approach his bed, and hold up the stump of a bleeding arm. The figure then disappeared. A period of 30 to 40 years were to pass and then it is told how Miss Tobias, then Mrs. T. S. Whitman, went to sit up with Mrs. Daley (who was not expected to live) at the Hillsdale. Their talk drifted to the supernatural, and Mrs. Daley asked Mrs. Whitman, "Do you believe in ghosts?" Mrs. Whitman said, "no," but Mrs. Daley added, "I do. Some years ago when we lived in the old Williams house" — and then recounted an experience exactly the same as the story told by George Ince.

Mrs. Whitman recalled the coincidence of her girlhood days. Other visitors of the Williamses, occupying the east spare bedroom, have seen the figure of this soldier. He was described as being tall and of splendid physique, wearing the uniform of the Royal Engineers. This uniform seemed to be somewhat torn and defaced, one shoulder strap being missing, and his helmet was thrown hack and hung suspended by the chin strap over the right shoulder. The clank of his spurs sounded on the floor as he approached the bed. As he drew near the paralyzed watcher, his face was seen to be deathly in hue, his eyes bulging and his face drawn as if in intense pain. He seemed to be searching for someone and in his left hand carried an unsheathed cavalry sword. Then it was he raised his bleeding arm severed at the wrist. There is a sequel. When digging the cellar for the Union (now Royal) Bank, a skeleton was found in a drain box. A lady looking out of her window at the time saw a man lift a plank and then run as if for his life. A crowd soon gathered, and Mr. Jack Ritchie, the first to arrive, exclaimed, "My G—, it is John Kennedy!" It seems that John Kennedy of Granville had disappeared and the only trace found of him was his hat, pierced by two bullets, floating upon the river. But this corpse, as shown by the clothing and brass buttons, was evidently that of a soldier. There were those who remembered an army pay officer having mysteriously disappeared, and more than likely this was his body. The story goes further, for although the body was quickly exhumed, it was noted that the right arm was cut off above the wrist. A young lady carried off the skull; the boots, sharp pointed ones, were in Judge Cowling's office for years. However, it was Mr. Gray who, seeing the excitement, went over to his store and from his collection of curios returned with these pointed shoes, which he dropped at the man's feet, unobserved. This ruse never leaked out. "The laying of the ghost" was an old saying which inferred that if the remains concerned were discovered the ghost appeared no more; however, the tenants of the Williams house for long after claimed "a queer feeling" persisted.

Joseph Norman, styled "Major" Norman, and his wife, later occupied the Williams house. He was the last ordnance keeper here, a bluff old soldier with an interesting career, having served faithfully under the Duke of Wellington in the Peninsular wars. Scarcely any history or even tourist pamphlet of the place fails to tell the romantic life of his Spanish wife, Gregoria Remona Antonia — attractive and interesting. She was a vivandiére on the battlefields when Wellington and Napoleon fought for supremacy. Being taken prisoner at one of the sieges, the Duke befriended her, had her married and sent to what was then very faraway Annapolis Royal. Major Norman's pension was £150 per year for life. She was a familiar figure on our streets, conspicuously dressed in bright colours and wearing a turban wound about her head. She liked to talk of "my dear Duke" to the ladies of the garrison, but to her husband, with whom she did not get on very well, it was "You Normena! You bruta beasta! You breaken my hearta, but what is worsen you breaken my crockery ware," from which jargon may be gathered that the crockery (meaning china) was valuable and a dear possession. Her hobby, or consolation, was in her pet dogs, four white French poodles, named Jacobena, Puppet, Malta Ray, and Tabby, and for whom she bought rabbits from the boys to feed them. When the household articles of the Normans were auctioned off, there were some beautiful pieces of English linen, jewellery, and silver, the last of which it is said bore the Wellington crest. Mrs. Norman always gave the "fixins" whenever a ball was given in the Assembly Hall.

Where Victoria Street enters St. George was once the home of the Winnietts. It is remembered as being a long, low quaint house in two parts and upstairs having "knees" for support like those in a small vessel. Becoming dilapidated, it was torn down in 1884. The Winnietts (Fr. Ouinette) represented the oldest English-speaking family in the Maritimes, and were prominent in everything relating to the town, establishing trade between Annapolis and Boston. This site of the birthplace of Sir Robert Winniett, one of a family of 12 children, is also marked by a tablet which was unveiled the same day as the Williams tablet. It reads:

On next lot south now merged in the street was born
March 2, 1793
Sir William Robert Wolseley Winniett
Knight, Captain, R.N.
Governor General Cape Coast District
Valiant Officer
Beneficent Administrator
———————————————————

NOVA SCOTIA HISTORICAL SOCIETY

In Calnek and Savary's *History* will be seen his poem of his native town and the relationship of these two old dwellings described: "Long these quaint old mansions, suggestive relics of other days and fashions, stood side by side, pathetic memorials of a generation of worthies long passed away and as if to perpetrate, if possible, the life-long and brotherly friendship that existed between their two owners."

The following story is taken with kind permission from In *Pioneer Days* (Dent Canadian History Readers) by Dr. D. J. Dickie, published by J. M. Dent & Sons, Limited.

In the gallant days when Port Royal was still French, Captain Baptiste was the most dangerous privateer who sailed the northern seas. Many a richly laden prize did he tow proudly into harbour. Boston merchants feared him as they did the devil himself; all who could took cover when word came down the wind that Captain Baptiste had slipped his cable. His home was the finest in Port Royal; his dinners the best, his wines the oldest, his daughters the prettiest. Half the gay doings of the town went on under his roof. The wild sea dogs who were his comrades sang, told stories in the kitchen, while the gay young officers from the fort danced with the girls in the parlour. Open house he kept, and never a night but someone knocked for food or fun.

Of the jolly company, Captain Baptiste's daughter, Marie Maisonat, was the gayest. Dark and slender, her flashing eyes dared everyone to follow her in each new prank her witty mind invented. Like her race, impulsive; like her father, utterly careless of consequences, she led the youth of old Port Royal in hunt, in tramp, in dance a merry chase.

When Nicholson came to Port Royal in 1710, there sailed in his company one William Winniett, Huguenot, who, when the Protestants were driven from France, had escaped to London and so to Boston. Winniett was an adventurous person. He had not been many weeks in Port Royal before he determined to have Marie, and have her he did. In a year's time they married, and Winniett, settling down to trade, became shortly the leading merchant and shipowner of Nova Scotia. So "Mad Marie" moved from one handsome home to another. But now her tricks and jokes were over. Her husband became a member of the Council of Annapolis Royal and the corn roasts and sleigh rides, the hunting and fishing picnics gave place to grand dinner parties where the governor was entertained in state and public policy discussed from soup to nuts.

One imagines Marie yawning behind her beringed fingers. But, no! Times had changed, and with them the versatile lady. Hunting and dancing were gone with her lost French youth; politics and power were come with the British. For Marie discovered that she loved power; knew how to win it; knew how to use it. The British government needed information about the woods, the streams, the Indians, the Acadians, Quebec, the Court of France. Marie had it or knew ways of getting it, and Marie was British now. Many a plot was revealed in her parlour, many a plan laid about her dinner table. Her great brown eyes shone with pride as she listened, suggested, advised, and with her woman's wit found ways to circumvent the enemy. Years passed; Marie grew old and stout. She forgot to care about velvets and jewels, about parties and beaux; but the love of power grew. In her drugget dress, large bonnet, and heavy garden shoes, she ruled Annapolis as she had ruled Port Royal. She married her daughters to British officers — the eldest, wife of Captain Cosby, Lieutenant-Governor of Annapolis; the second one became the wife of Lieutenant Handfield; and the third was married to Captain Edward Howe, whom Le Loutre was accused of shooting. Grandsons and granddaughters grew up 'round Marie, fine stalwart young fellows and pretty girls. These, too, she married into important families; so she kept her power.

The private soldiers, when not on guard, were kept busy patching up the tumbling walls. Sometimes one or other of them would get a job helping some merchant in the town and so earn sixpence. Too often, then, the careless fellows dropped into a tavern to spend it, and being called to account by their superior officers would always reply: "I was called to finish a job for Madame Winniett." The officer might storm, but he could do nothing, for Marie never permitted anyone to invoke her name in vain. If the sinner were ordered "confined to barracks," she ordered him to be released and the officer was obliged to let him go. Soon after Captain Knox arrived in Port Royal he was taken by a friend to call on Madame Winniett. They saw in her drawing-room a tall young fellow — her grandson. He was well dressed in the uniform of an officer's servant. Knox stared at his hat, thinking it rude of him not to take it off to them. The poor lad was an imbecile, but they did not know that. Seeing Knox stare, the old lady became offended and said she could assure him that the boy was an officer's son and as good as he was. Knox, not meaning any harm, said he supposed he was the son of a French militia man. At this, Madame fell into a towering rage and shouted out: "We have rendered King Shorge more important services dan ever you did or peut-être (perhaps) ever shall; and dis be well known to people en authorité." As she grew more and more angry, Knox and his friend thought it was time to decamp. They slipped out, leaving her to vent her temper on her grandson.

Across the street, where the lighthouse now stands, was the Government House, a large two and a half storey wooden building which was burned in 1833. The circumstances were as follows: A captain with a surgeon and lieutenant had gone to a party, leaving an orderly in charge. While the latter went off to the barracks for a good time, sparks from the open fireplace set fire to the floor and made such headway that all efforts to save the building were futile. All the officers had left were the clothes in which they stood. A china mug, the only relic preserved to this day, was brought out by Captain Bush. We are indebted to Judge Savary for the gateposts, and for the small bronze tablets, which read:

This lot is
the site of the old
Government House
Residence of the chief military officer
Destroyed by fire in 1833

The birthplace of
Sir Charles Henry Darling
1809-1870
who ably served the Empire as
Governor of important colonies.

In passing the firm of Wm. McCormick and Sons (which had its 75th anniversary) we come to a group of very old buildings but all have been modernized. What was a small cottage with shop adjoining, belonging to Mr. J. W. Shannon, has been enlarged and the house is now the home of Mrs. Frank Orde, while the shop is Banks' Hardware. Mr. Shannon kept a dry goods and millinery business in the days when there were little or no ready-to-wear clothes. He was the best of citizens and is remembered for the efficient manner in which he carried out his part in the programmes for various celebrations.

The last and smallest building was known as Brimstone Corner, so named from the discussions of some of those men who frequented it —Foxy Bill, Red Top, Konky (the last always spoke in a high shrill voice reminding one of the sound heard in a conch shell). Here Clarey Ritchie had her famous candy store, which meant, principally, one-foot-length molasses sticks. The post office too was in this locality at one time, when the one mail bag was carried on a man's back.

Mr. H. Wear's residence is on the site of an old landmark, the Foster House, latterly called Clifton House. The Fosters built it as a boarding house but they also had a shop, a ladies' emporium, managed by the three energetic daughters. One daughter, Miss Susan, afterwards built Hillsdale.

Judge Haliburton House

Until his recent death Dr. J. A. M. Hemmeon owned the Haliburton House, which was built by a soldier named Gallagher, of the fort, in 1808, and was a fine residence in its day. It is of special historical significance, having been the home of Judge Haliburton for eight years. Here several of his 10 children were born and three of them sleep in the old churchyard. Judge Haliburton was called to the Bar in 1820 and practiced law in Annapolis and wrote several of his books here. He became a judge at 32 years of age and he then removed to Windsor. The centennial of his citizenship here was celebrated in 1921 when a brass tablet was unveiled and is now in Fort Anne Museum. Later this house belonged to Judge Cowling. We can imagine it as a great meeting place for the literati of the town.

Where Chan's Restaurant now operates stood the American House, formerly the large home of Mr. and Mrs. Alfred Whitman and their three sons and daughters.

One would think Longfellow had Annapolis Royal in mind when he wrote of the "fort, the wooden houses quaint and brown," for that certainly applied to the small row of homes facing the fort known as Pension Row. This name arose from the many widows and mothers of deceased soldiers who lived there. One among them was the widow of Lieutenant Walker. Lieutenant Walker (40th Regiment) was in receipt of the "Penderel Pension" which had been granted by King Charles II in perpetuity to the descendants of "trusty Dick Penderel" of whom Lieutenant Walker was one. So well and faithfully did Penderel perform his duty and so great was Charles's gratitude that his family were honoured by court notice and a government position.

Another of these houses, on the corner of St. James Street, is well remembered as a very quaint low rambling house. It had two very large willow trees at one side, a fine fruit and vegetable garden at the rear, and a smaller garden in the front with a paling fence (there was the usual encroachment upon the sidewalk). Here grew syringa, multi-flora rose, and ivy at random. What mattered if they covered the windows? Sunshine was not considered of much account in those days. The walls outside and inside were painted in red ochre; the floors at the back sloped like the deck of a ship; upstairs there were spooky looking corners, notably the dark slave room, and it took much courage to even peep in for us, as children. The furniture was of Chippendale and Empire designs, and for more than 100 years it was the home of the Runcimans and the Brittains. A new building replaced the old house when it was torn down in 1897, but it was destroyed in the big fire of 1921.

Doorway Of Dunvegan House

It seems to have been uppermost in the minds of the townspeople to cater to the officers of the fort. What we used to know as the Queen Hotel was built by John McLeod, a merchant of Halifax, for use as a store and residence but also for the accommodation of the officers. It was named Dunvegan after the oldest still inhabited castle in Skye, Scotland. The clan McLeod is the owner. Dunvegan was modernized and enlarged from time to time but finally succumbed to the flames in the fire of 1921. Some pretty features of this house were the windows of Colonial bow-shape, fan and sidelights of the doorway, mahogany stair-rail and newel post, the arched doorways, etc. (Two of these windows have been preserved and are in the present Golf Club house of today.) In the basement were the wine and vegetable rooms and spring for domestic uses. Latterly it was the rendezvous for political gatherings and on days like "Declaration" there would be a big dinner given by the winning side. On these occasions, it was Major Millidge Harris's chief delight to carve from the side table in the dining room from an abundance of goose, chicken, and beef, followed by mince pies and plum pudding, which usually composed the menu. The big brick oven was heated many times in preparation for these events. Chicken then sold for 25 cents each and geese at 50 cents each. Someone reported that there was money or buried treasure in the north corner of the cellar and so excavations went on so often that they had to be stopped, lest the walls should fall. Following the McLeods, the Foster family moved and took up residence there. The Foster girls, quite naturally, long held a hope of attaching an officer; but alas for their cherished dreams! On the day when the garrison made their final exit in 1854 they were seen in the window weeping copiously. Old "Andy" Gilmour (last remaining soldier) looked up and said, "Never mind girls, you'll get a soldier yet someday." Poor consolation when an officer was their ambition. Dunvegan got its later name Queen Hotel in 1891 from John McLeod, who became its proprietor.

When "Antie" Reynolds kept the next house, which was a tavern, in which the score tablets showing the number of drinks allotted to the soldiers were prominently displayed, the following story originated: A soldier foraging for provisions in the store made his entrance by way of the chimney — not like those of today — but took the wrong side and got in the flue just as the family fire was being lighted. Hearing the groanings and imprecations, they were surprised to find a man pinioned there. Immediately a rope was lowered and he was taken out, only a little the worse for being smoked.

We first hear of the Harrises in one John Harris who was living here in 1755 and owned a large property on Runciman's Corner. When John Harris was attending the Assembly in Halifax, there were two invitations extended to him by the Earl of Dalhousie, Governor of Nova Scotia, about 1818. They read:

The Earl of Dalhousie
Requests the honour of
Mr. Harris's Company at Dinner
On Tuesday the 17th, February
at five and a half o'clock
An answer is requested,
and

The Countess of Dalhousie
Requests the honour of Mr. Harris's Company
On Friday evening, the 24th April
at 9 o'clock.

The firm of Price and Co. is now on the Runciman Corner, where the Runcimans had four stores on the same spot at different times, as one by one fire destroyed them. The business lived for more than 100 years under the name of Glasgow House. A story is told of one of the firm, George Runciman, concerning the time he was leaving Scotland about 1800. He said to the woman who was standing near him on the wharf: "Anent the matter we were speaking on Belle, are ye agreed?" She said, "Aye, Geordie, I am agreed." "Alricht an," he replied. That was the betrothal. The climax was her coming here and their marriage.

For quite a stretch, from this point there were no buildings — the land being government property. The residence of Miss Lilian B. Johnson was one of the many removed to make way for the Windsor & Annapolis Railway (1862). It was willed to Miss Mary Roach from her brother W. H. Roach, MPP, and is about 150 years old.

Colonel Fred Sinclair's farm, which extended from the Court House to Mr. Bank's residence, had formerly belonged to the La Tours and then passed into the hands of Judge Ritchie and his successors. The house known later as the Methodist Mission House, the second oldest existing, stood where the present United Church stands. Later this property was divided and on it was built the Church of England rectory by Rev. J. J. Ritchie. The fine old house and grounds is now the home of the Roy Smiths. It was also the home of Mrs. Borden until her death. Mrs. Borden was the widow of the late Dr. B. C. Borden, for a long time president of Mount Allison University.

The house on the left, second above the bridge, was built on an old French cellar by Peter Bonnett, High Sheriff for 26 years, in anticipation of a family. There was none. However, an adopted daughter had five children who grew up there. It has been sadly changed in many respects. It had a doorway of excellent design, Gothic windows with shutters, and a stairway which led to a roof that was circled by a railing and overlaid with copper. The furnishings were beautiful, with wonderful old mahogany, old china, and silver, and these treasures, acquired at the time of their marriage, lasted for over half a century. Mrs. Elizabeth Bailey Bonnett was the granddaughter of both the Rev. Jacob Bailey and Colonel James DeLancey. Included in her silver was a coffee pot that belonged to Colonel DeLancey, the one in which his female slave made coffee and poisoned him. He died from the effects of the poison, in 1804. He had foolishly promised her her freedom when he died and it seems she took this way to be sure of her release. The garden came to be looked upon as a place for hidden treasure, digging going on about the trees, as Mr. Bonnett was known to have had money. There being no banks in town; valuables and surplus money were naturally secreted. Only recently a gentleman of the town told the following tale, prefacing the story with "I saw with my own eyes." It seems that a man was plowing at the rear of the house with a team of oxen, when one of the oxen went down to its haunches. The teamster was instantly dismissed. So that was where the treasure was! Spanish doubloons and French coins were unearthed, so it is claimed. The story continues as to how the owner of the house had his wife make him a belt for the money and that he then went to Boston and exchanged the find for American currency. "This person seemed to have money which he never had before, and in what other way could he have gotten it?" the narrator concluded. The accompanying picture shows the house as it was originally and makes us wish that restoration was possible, as might be said of several others. A peacock strutting about the grounds completed the pretty picture.

Peter Bonnett House

Nearby is the Roy Smith apartment house, formerly the home of our historian Judge Savary, and stands on the site of Governor Phillips's residence. It was built by Captain DeLap, who did a big shipbuilding business, and was always known by its tulip tree — the only one in town. The house, a pretty low-roofed building, so low that one could easily touch the eaves, had deep casement windows and hand-carved mantels. The tragedy of Mrs. J. Johnston, who once lived here, is recorded elsewhere.

The pretty little vine-clad cottage of Lieutenant Newton, who lived here in the latter part of the eighteenth century, is not recognizable in the Queen Hotel Annex, it having undergone many additions and improvements. When Dr. Leslie of Edinburgh, Scotland, surgeon to the British Army, came out here as surgeon to the garrison force, he, with his young family, took up his abode in the barracks. They afterwards removed to the Newton cottage and lived there as the "family doctor" of the town with their six boys and six girls. Dentistry or, correctly speaking, teeth extraction, was also part of his profession, a description of which has been related thus: The head was held in position, then formidable-looking forceps, or a large key having a wooden handle and steel frame, was applied and with the injunction "don't laff," the tooth was given a rough wrench, regardless of whether a piece of the jaw bone might come with it or not. Dr. Leslie's daughters were leaders in fashion. They had the smallest waists and wore the largest hoop skirts. It has been told how a young curate accompanying them down the street was compelled to take the ditch in order to allow space for these voluminous monstrosities.

Such girls did not go away to earn their living, as it was considered "infra dig," but perhaps they would teach in a private school. In the case of one of Dr. Leslie's daughters, she gave dancing lessons, no doubt because she was considered graceful. Polka redowas, mazurkas, and cotillions would be the popular dances. We think of this same house in the days when Judge and Mrs. Owen lived there, with its beautiful furnishings, when it was the centre of hospitality. No one of any note visited the town without being entertained by them.

Hob Fireplace

The large and lovely property of Dr. J. R. Kerr originally belonged to George Millidge, a lawyer, son of the Rev. John Millidge. Looking back today, it is remembered as the home of Mr. and Mrs. George Corbitt and family, Mr. Corbitt having acquired it at the age of 21 and retained it until his death in his 91st year. A very comfortable house, it has suffered changes both inside and outside. Nearly all places in this locality had an apple orchard either in front or back of the house or both, and this was true of this house. Mr. Corbitt devoted much time to gardening, rose culture being his specialty. An old-timer claimed this property had a thick row of spruce trees lining the highway, which kept the street wet, and of how the schoolchildren would stop and pick spruce gum.

The Rev. John Millidge, D.C.L., rector of St. Luke's Church, built the Runciman house — the finest example of Georgian Colonial architecture we have — and it stood nearly as we see it today in its fine setting of old trees and lawns. The interior is unchanged; the fine large rooms, pretty enclosed and winding staircase, large open fireplaces, and even the kitchen, where hangs the crane that once was used for the daily cooking. The lovely garden at the rear enhances the attractiveness of the place. It was named Girvan Bank.

Runciman House

Two hundred and forty years is a very long time, but such is said to be the age of one house, the oldest of all, now owned by Mrs. A. W. Banks. The walls are filled with clay between the studding, from the sills to the gambrel roof. There are wide chimney abutments built of stone and floors of plank 14 to 18 inches wide that never shrunk. All timber and joists in the upper part of the house are 11 by 11 inches. It has two roofs, one 18 inches above the other, with the double purpose of making the house warmer in winter and cooler in summer. The original clapboards were fastened with wrought handmade nails, heads the size of ten-cent pieces. Dormer windows and ell are more recent additions. Formerly slave quarters and kitchen were at the rear of the house.

Oldest House
(Residence of Mrs. A. W. Banks)

It was the home of many prominent families, notably the DeLanceys and Barclays. Here Colonel DeLancey gave a reception for His Royal Highness the Duke of Kent on the occasion of his first visit to Annapolis Royal. The late Mrs. J. M. Owen wrote: "A resident of Annapolis Royal says she heard her mother say she remembered her mother dressing to go to this reception 'to see the King's royal son.' Besides her own toilette, she made ready a pretty maid, who was to assist in the waiting. Either the becoming dress or the girl's own beauty, perhaps a combination of the two, attracted the prince, for — undignified in a scion of royalty and scandalous to chronicle — H.R.H. His Royal Highness] was caught behind one of Colonel DeLancey's doors kissing the pretty waiting maid."

When Colonel Barclay, ordnance and storekeeper of the garrison, was dismissed from his office (because on the second visit of the Duke of Kent he would not call on Madame St. Laurent who was travelling with the Duke as his so-called morganatic wife), James Fraser of Fredericton was ordered to take his place. He and his widowed daughter, Mrs. (Captain) Thong, then took over the Barclay homestead. Dr. Henkell — to give him his full name, George Christian Conrad Gasper Henkell — Staff Surgeon to the Duke of Kent, came here and later married Mrs. Thong. Captain Thong had had a watch that saved his life from a bullet. His widow passed it down from brother to brother until it came into the possession of the late Dr. Robinson. Now, the good doctor was vain, and he looked upon the watch as being more like a small frying pan, so, failing to wear it, the memento became lost. Prince Edward and Dr. Henkell were great friends as they used to sit and talk in German over their pipes and beer. When the Prince left Annapolis Royal, he presented Dr. Henkell's son, Edward, with a sword having a carved ivory hilt. It was given to Dr. Robinson by his uncle and is now in the Dominion Archives at Ottawa. At dinner with the Duke of Kent, Dr. Henkell absent-mindedly drew out his snuff box and was taking a pinch when he suddenly remembered the presence of His Royal Highness. Thinking it was a breach of etiquette, he made a vow never to take snuff again. Shortly thereafter he died from a bleeding spell; the result, it was said, of not taking snuff!

At that time there was no house between the Barclay home and The Gables, and when the Tobias girls lived in the

Barclay house they would arrange to signal their neighbours at the Gables by means of a code, employing handkerchiefs at the upper windows if they wished to visit them.

Mrs. Barclay was said to have been cruel to her slaves. These stories are likely exaggerated, yet there must have been some foundation for them. Some slave owners are reputed to have thought severe punishment necessary. There have been accounts of slaves tied by their thumbs in the attic, of a slave girl stealing pie and being made to crawl into the hog pen, retrieve and eat the crust she had thrown there. The most horrifying story concerns a slave murdered and sealed up in a fireplace, and this last is supposed to account for the ghost claimed to be that of Mrs. Barclay. Occupants of the Barclay house have declared they have seen in the bedroom a woman wearing a checkered shawl rocking herself.[3]

Now we come to the two hotels — the Queen Hotel and the Hillsdale House — both having interesting histories. The former, known as the Ritchie House, was built by Mr. William Ritchie on the anticipation of a fortune being left him in England, but which never materialized. The contract was given out for $13,000, but before the contractor had gone very far, he failed, and then the town firm of Pickels & Mills took it over and completed it. This house, set in large grounds, was to be for his only child, Norman, who had recently married pretty Fanny O'Dell. Think of such a home for a young couple! Long before it was finished, young

[3] Proof that the Barclay and Tobias families lived in this particular house is found on windowpanes in two of the upstairs rooms. On one of the small panes in an upstairs window is scratched (upside down) "Lt. Barclay, R.M. Reg," and in another room, on two panes of a window have been written "George Tobias" and "Louisa Tobias." These were evidently done with a diamond.

Mrs. Norman Ritchie (20) died after only 10 months of married life. An old letter of that time read: "Mr. William Ritchie is building a mansion and making himself a poor man."

Mr. Ritchie had married Fanny Foster, sister to Mrs. Ryerson of the Hillsdale. Perhaps accentuated by a bit of rivalry, he built in a more pretentious manner, pushing the ceilings a little higher, making a larger staircase, doors and windows finished in heavy oak mouldings, anything that would make it appear on a grander scale. It was complete throughout in the best Victorian style. In the large and substantial cellar was a water tank to supply the water to kitchen and on the third floor another for bath and bedrooms — small marble basins being set in box-like compartments. A fancy iron grille work ran around the roof and a doorbell that could not be obtained in Canada had to be cast in Philadelphia. A balustrade fence having gates at either end of driveway enclosed the property.

Mr. Ritchie, who had a reputation for "being fond of lawsuits," right here became involved in one. He said the house was not according to specifications and refused to take it over. Being in state of liquidation, the public roamed through it at will. Finally it was settled, which ended in his paying only $1,000 for it and at that he had put in all he had. The story goes of a lawsuit between Mr. Ritchie and Mr. Matthew Ritchie concerning an apple (pippin) tree, the branches of which hung over on the other's property. The case was in court so many times, and costly, that finally the judge, getting weary of it, said: "For heaven's sake, call it by some other name than a pippin tree!"

Then Mr. and Mrs. Ritchie kept a private boarding house, catering to the "best families" both outside the town as well as in. With large airy rooms and no central heating for winter, the many grates had to be kept well supplied with coal and wood — both of which were cheap and plentiful.

Mr. Ritchie also ran a stagecoach between here and Caledonia — 42 miles distant.

After Mr. and Mrs. Ritchie and son, Norman, had passed on, various parties took it over, but it never proved a success. At one time it was the Baptist parsonage, Rev. Coulter White being pastor, when it rented for the exorbitant price of $25 a month! Then it was left vacant, the only occupant being the life-sized stuffed moose standing in the hall, which Norman had shot.

Another phase in the history of this house was the opening of a private school for boys in 1897. (See Schools.) When that closed, again it was left desolate.

Then a Mrs. McInnes bought it and thereby hangs a tale — a "once upon a time" one. When a little girl, Clara Sabeans by name, slim and blonde, and most likely in tattered dress, bare feet in summer, for her parents were very poor, she used to watch the grand Ritchie house grow and wish she could own it someday — a dream she never lost sight of. The Sabeans then lived in a small old house on Academy Square. Clara helped to eke out a living by selling mushrooms, marsh greens, etc., or by begging. She would say at someone's door that she had two or three cents to buy a loaf of bread and could she get a few more, or a few cents to go on the ferry to Granville. She never missed out on anything in town and became intensely interested in watching Mr. W. W. Clarke swim in the Annapolis River. He kindly gave her lessons and under his tutelage she soon became a proficient swimmer. When about 17 years old, Clara went to Boston on the steamer Hunter that plied between here and that port. At the beaches there she attracted attention by her stunts and fearlessness in the water, which led up to her being asked to become a performer in the Boston American Swimming Pool. Then a company was formed and she was taken to all the large cities in the USA as Clara Beckwith, the champion swimmer. Besides this profession and with her fine figure, she became a model for sculptors. This was corroborated by Mr. Clarke, who, on going into the Washington, DC, Art Gallery and looking up, exclaimed, "Why, there's Clara!" Occasionally she visited her native town in the summer and never forgot Mr. Clarke's kindness. Some years passed and then it was known that she had married Mr. McInnes, MP, Minister of Education for Manitoba, and that he had died, leaving her a wealthy widow.

One day there was quite a flutter in town, for Clara was coming back to fulfil her dream — to buy the Ritchie house. She brought a friend with her, also a lot of baggage. She called the place The Old Orchard House, from the old orchard to the south of it, and began to get ready for tourists. Business boomed in the old town, for she ordered all the best furnishings the merchants could provide — but with promissory payments.

Her house in order, she gave a large reception one evening, and with her friend, graciously received her guests; a large French music box played, while refreshments were served in the dining room. How did the townspeople react? There were those who scoffed — "wouldn't think of going," knowing her background. Some went for business reasons, some out of curiosity, while others just to be neighbourly — for hadn't she come to live amongst us?

The tourist season was slim that summer, not what she had anticipated, and she had spent considerable money on the place. So, with her resources running low, she suddenly decided to decamp. One evening, she called up the firm of Chas. Dargie & Son, telling them they could have the furniture back as it was just as good as when she bought it. The next morning word quickly got around that she was leaving town and bills not paid! One of her creditors got out a capias, but not soon enough for Clara, for when the policeman arrived with it at the station she was already on the train, waving a calm and smiling goodbye. The merchants afterwards recovered most of their goods.

This was the end of Clara as far as Annapolis Royal was concerned.

Mrs. McInnes had asked Mr. Will Mills, one of the firm who had built the house, to buy it. This he did in 1909, including a piano and Mr. McInnes's library. Mr. Mills, finding it too large for a small family, sold it again to Mr. Amey of the USA. In 1921, the year of the big fire in town, the old Queen Hotel was burned. The then proprietor, Mr. W. C. McPherson, in looking around for a place, was able to buy this one, and that is how the Queen Hotel is uptown today.

Mr. and Mrs. W. C. McPherson kept a first-class hotel and, on their deaths, their daughter Jean and her husband, Mr. W.C. Crosby, took it over and have built up a fine business, accommodation being limited most of the time. In need of more bedrooms, the fine residence of the late Mr. J. M. Owen was acquired — now known as The Annex. The building at the rear houses the help, but the main house has never changed, with the exception of some modern conveniences. Today it is a favourite place for all travellers.

Something like 85 years have passed over the Hillsdale House. The Foster daughters (3), as before noted, kept a ladies' emporium — fine millinery, manteaux, china, etc. Now, one of the daughters, young Miss Susan, energetic and prosperous, wished to branch out on a further adventure. She bought the land known as the exercising ground for the soldiers of the fort, a quarter of a mile away, which extended from the main street (St. George) to the Allain River at the back, 11 acres in all. There she built her fine house of 25 rooms, besides store rooms, and a large carriage house attached, set well back from the road on spacious grounds. She named it the Hillsdale for, as she said, it had a dale to the front of it and a dale to the back of it. The barn — but why mention a barn, as every place had one? — was a fine structure too, complete with weather vane. In the basement of it was the hennery, having a glassed-in sunroom for the winter months. Next to it was the piggery with workshop above it. They were remarkable for the distance from the house. The beasts seem to have had more consideration given to them than man, for they could easily run out to pasturage on the marsh, while the milk pails had to be carried up the steep hill and then to the house. There was also an attractive small building on the slope of the hill for ice and a never-failing spring as now, of clear sparkling water — the water used for all purposes before the town supply was put in. The property had a fancy picket fence with large gateways in front as all of the places were enclosed then.

The house completed, Miss Foster was married in the double parlours to Mr. Edwin Ryerson, of Upper Clements. Together they worked hard and made a beautiful place of it, but it is remembered that she always assumed the leadership in all matters. It was said of Mr. Ryerson that he attended all the auctions and in time their house was filled with furniture, many of the pieces being rare antiques which they continued to collect. They planted many kinds of fruit trees — pears, quinces, plums, cherries, large grape vines, currants (said to have been a quarter of a mile of them), and a large apple orchard, which began at the front and extended on one side to the hill at the back, and another smaller one on the other side. Also, shrubbery and flowers were grown — a "wedding-cake" flower bed[4] being in front of the house. From these fruits Mrs. Ryerson made quantities of jams, jellies, and wines, which she sold. Mr. Ryerson used to say: "Give her a barrel of sugar, ditto of fruit, and she was happy."

Here they catered to first-class tourists in the summer, people coming then by boat and train. A little girl on answering the doorbell one day was met by a lady and gentleman seeking accommodation. She answered them that they kept only nice people there. On being assured that they were nice people, they were allowed to enter. This standard has been maintained throughout its history.

The oldest register dating back to 1870 contains many distinguished and interesting names — notably that of the late King George V, then Prince of Wales, and suite (4) from HMS Canada, who were there in June, 1884, and went on a fishing trip. The following is a story taken from the Spectator

---

[4] A wedding-cake flower bed, as the name suggests, resembled a wedding cake, having three tiers and spaced proportionately. About 20 feet in diameter, the sides were covered with greenswards. Flowers such as roses and peonies grew on the edges, leaving a space to walk between it and the next tier. It was approached at one side by steps. These flower beds were considered a very elegant addition to a front lawn but required a lot of care to keep up and have long since disappeared.

of that time: "When Mr. Dargie acted as guide, the old gentleman knew he belonged to Royalty or held an honourable position of some kind in the world, yet didn't know just how to address him. After stumbling over all the high-sounding titles he could think of, such as Your Majesty, Prince, My Lord, etc., he was lost in bewilderment. The Prince, noticing his embarrassment, wishing to set him at ease, said calmly, "Oh, just call me George." To which the old man replied, "Damn it, sonny, I think you're right."

As is the case with persons of note, his every action was noticed and the townspeople soon knew that he greased his own boots! The seat he placed under the quince trees and the coconut dipper from which he used to drink at the spring have long since gone.

Mrs. Ryerson liked to boast of the fact that she then had 13 kinds of wine in her wine cellar, which she invited the Prince to sample. He marvelled that one woman could do so much. After he got back to England, he sent her photographs of himself and party. These hung for years in the parlour of the Hillsdale, but latterly the photo of His Highness was stolen. On applying for another, her request was granted.

When the Marquis of Lansdowne, Governor General of Canada, Lady Lansdowne and suite, were there in 1884, Mrs. Ryerson gave them and their servants the complete run of the house. Mrs. E. McClafferty remembers going with her mother to hear the town band serenade them and their playing "Will Ye No Come Back Again."

In the same year, Lieutenant General Lord and Lady Alexander Russell, stationed at Halifax, came there to visit, arriving in a grand barouche and pair, coachman and footman.

Mrs. Ryerson seems to have had the priority on all the judges who came to town from the many listed in this same old register.

It has always been a popular resort and, at that time, the only attractive place outside of Halifax. The entertainment was not in swimming nor cars but very modest games and tennis, for which there was a court at the side of the house. Then there was the Mound, as now, a high promontory — probably an outpost in the early days of Port Royal — where guests enjoyed resting on warm summer days under the clump of large old spruce trees amidst the lovely setting of countryside, river, and mountains.

One of the first town bands was named after the Hillsdale. Mrs. Ryerson had an autograph quilt made containing names of many of her guests, which was afterwards sold and receipts given to the band. Then, too, her only and much beloved nephew, Norman Ritchie, was a popular cornet player in it.

Mrs. Ryerson and the Perkinses, of the old Queen Hotel, had been very good friends, and now in her declining days — Mr. Ryerson having predeceased her — she asked them to consider buying the place, which they did. In October, 1897, Mr. and Mrs. Cyrus A. Perkins and family moved in, just at the time when the apples (mostly nonpareils) were being picked, and there were perhaps 100 barrels that year.

Mrs. Ryerson lies buried in the old military cemetery beside her parents, her sisters, Fanny and Charlotte, and brothers John and Joseph, all in a row in the family lot.

All this is a background for the youngest member of the family, Mr. William Perkins, the present proprietor, who has been living there for more than 50 years.

Mr. and Mrs. Cyrus Perkins ran it on much the same lines as Mrs. Ryerson did. In those days food, both fish and fowl, was plentiful besides the produce from the place itself. Servants, too, one might say, were plentiful; if not satisfactory, they could be dismissed and others found to take their places.

The most distinguished people who stayed there in their time were many guests during the Tercentenary celebration in June, 1904: Vice Admiral Sir Archibald Douglas and party of the HMS *Ariadne*, and others from different parts of the world. Such delicacies as broiled lobsters and roast turkey were served, and the last of Susan Ryerson's wine, orange and raisin, clear and sparkling as champagne, was dispensed to this company. Also, at the bicentenary in 1910, commemorating the first Church of England Services in all Canada, were more noted visitors present.

Mr. and Mrs. Perkins in their time had built on some additional rooms; also three bungalows were erected on the grounds.

When Mr. and Mrs. Perkins had both passed on, the place was taken over by William, their youngest son, who had had winters of experience in hotel-keeping in Florida. He and his wife (nee Caroline Orde) have made many alterations and improvements in the house, more private baths installed and a large stone veranda built on the front. More antiques have been added, so that today it has many lovely and valuable pieces. Among the distinguished visitors of their time have been the late Lord Tweedsmuir, Governor General of Canada, 1937, and Prime Minister Mackenzie King. The house, catering to summer tourists, as a foremost hostelry is so well known that it is hardly necessary to tell of its attractions, the perfection of its appointments or its cuisine which naturally draws many visitors.

Close by is the residence of Mr. R. A. Laurence, built by Rev. H. D. de Blois, D.C.L. It, too, is set on spacious grounds, formerly part of the Judge Ritchie property. The Rev. de Blois saw to it that its structure was of the very best of that period, the mid-Victorian style, having a carriage house attached and now, as usual, the garage.

By far the finest of all the places was The Grange, the home of Judge Thomas Ritchie, where the Annapolis Royal Academy now stands. It was a fine Colonial house, built about the year 1810 and alluded to in old writings as "the mansion." It had three stories and basement; in the latter were servants' hall, dairy with pump room, and kitchens. On the main floor were double parlours with bedroom, library, dining room, and butler's pantry. An ascending, winding stairway led to seven bedrooms, with a further four on the uppermost floor or attic. In the winter it was heated by a large iron hall stove which burnt half cordwood sticks, while in all the rooms were fireplaces. The residence proper was beautifully situated on one acre of land with fine trees as now. The oak trees along the street were planted with acorns sent from Smyrna by Captain Lightenstone, grandfather of Mrs. Eliza Ritchie. The big elms in front of the house were carried as saplings in front of Mr. J. Johnstone (brother of Mrs. Ritchie) as he rode on his horse from somewhere in Kings County. In summer the foliage was so thick that the many outbuildings could not be seen. The school bell is the same as that which first rang in St. Luke's Church, for Judge Ritchie took it in exchange for a new one, using the old bell to summon his farm labourers to work. Surrounded by a high hawthorn hedge, it embraced all that land from Mr. A. L. MacKenzie's and back as far as the river. Judge Ritchie kept a large establishment, herds of cattle and sheep, for he had a farm locally as well as one outside of the town. The old saying that "Annapolis Royal belonged to Judge Ritchie, the church and the devil" leads one to believe that he was great in power and possessions.

The Grange

When he travelled to Halifax as Member, he went in his big barouche, which his wife also used for riding about the town.

The old people used to say "Oh, that garden!" They spoke of the wonderful garden across the street, the like of which was not known elsewhere in the province. The entrance to it was by an arbour, where the house owned by Mr. Leslie Murphy and occupied by Mr. L. Hersey now is. It was locked during the week but remained open for visitors on Sundays. Three terraces with steps connecting joined the entrance and led to a rose-bordered walk, surrounded by a high hawthorn hedge, and ran well back of the other now existing properties.

At the spring, called St. Cyprian's, the family washing was done in summer. From *Recollections of a Georgia Loyalist* in reference to the spring, the following appears: "We helped Eliza, especially on wash day, a grand event, which occurred once a fortnight in every family, at which all the servants assisted." There was also a farmhouse at the foot of the terraces and nearby were a quince orchard, grape vines, nut trees, and almost every fruit that would grow in this climate. We may conclude that this was the part designated as Sampson's Hollow. Traces of the old terraces may still be seen, while flowers, such as daffodils and hyacinths that come up in the spring and the roses of June, still bloom as though defying the hand of time to pluck them out.

The family of Judge Ritchie and their life is most interesting. He had three wives; the first one being Elizabeth, daughter of William Martin Johnstone, a beautiful character, if one may judge from the epitaph on her large recumbent stone in the old cemetery. She died in 1819 at the age of 32, leaving seven children, "too young to feel their loss." Amongst her sons were Judge John Ritchie; Sir William Johnstone Ritchie, Chief Justice of Canada; and Rev. J. J. Ritchie, nearly 30 years rector of St. Luke's Church. To this family of orphaned children, besides a grandmother and two nieces, came the second wife, Elizabeth Best, sister of the rector of Fredericton. She was a good-natured, indulgent stepmother and got her own way quietly. The following story is told of her: Miss Best and a party, while walking on a moor in Yorkshire, England, met a gypsy. They all had their fortunes told and Miss Best's went thus: "You will cross the water, marry a widower with children, and be married with two rings." Miss Best remarked to her friends, "Your fortunes may come true, mine won't. I hate the sea so much that I refused to visit Ireland and I would not look at a widower with children." Later she changed her mind on both points, her sister being responsible for the first, and Judge Ritchie on the other. On the wedding day a Saint John friend, who was to buy the ring and bring it, failed to appear. A ring was borrowed for the occasion and returned the next day, when the belated friend turned up. She lived for some years but had no children of her own to survive her. She died as the result of injuries received following a fall from her horse.

The third wife was Anne, nicknamed "Queen Anne," daughter of Colonel Joseph Norman Bond, Yarmouth, by whom there were two children, the last being Judge Norman Ritchie, father of Mrs. F. C. Whitman. When Judge Ritchie died, the Grange passed into other hands until, in 1878, it was purchased for the Annapolis Royal Academy. The old building, being past its usefulness, was torn down (1902).

In its palmy days as a place of social functions, it had been unrivalled. The judge dispensed hospitality from here in great style, having plenty of servants and all the best that the land afforded. We can imagine the pure linen, the solid silver that graced the dinners, the old soup tureen, the large game platters that are now relegated to the topmost pantry shelves or to parlour tables as antiques. Sometimes there were suppers with whist later; but best of all, was the big "Popularity Ball" given once a year, when everyone was invited, dancing being done to the tune of a coloured fiddler or two. Whips and charlotte russe (the more fruitcake and wine in it the better) were some of the dainty dishes passed around. A lady used to tell how, when at a party there one night, and joined by the Judge, he asked her if she would have another half orange — evidently a treat in those days.

It was from Mrs. (Haliburton) Brown that the pen picture of the Ritchie garden came. It was she who told of the preparations in the servants' hall for the winters — how they would gather evenings, shell corn, fill bins with nuts, string barrels of dried apples, stow squash on shelves, etc. We like to let our imagination see it as it was in those days when it was owned by a man of such character and force of the fine old school, from whose family more lawyers and judges have sprung than any other in Canada. He died in 1852, aged 75. In the words of the Calnek and Savary *History*: "Few men had greater influence in the community in which he lived and still fewer knew how to exert such an influence so wisely and so well."

The Haliburtons succeeded the Ritchies and then a family of Willeys bought the place. Mr. Willey, a retired lawyer of Boston, of the distinguished Lithgow family, came here for his health and brought with him many beautiful things. On Mr. Willey's death there was an auction which lasted a week. Mr. E. Ryerson then purchased the property and when he went to the Hillsdale took three of the nice mantels with him. Then finally it passed into the School Commissioner's hands, as already noted.

Houses beyond this were few and far between; there was one on the Gilliatt property belonging to the LeCains and Corbitts — the Mrs. O. Logan house, the home of the Gilpins called The Rest, then as the James Fraser house. Later it was owned by Sheriff Cutler and others, while at present it is in the hands of Mr. P. G. Adams. Set among lovely old trees and lawns, it has undergone several changes. At the rear were servants' quarters and, from the wharf on the estate, Mr. Fraser shipped cordwood on the vessel *Seepter* to Saint John, the ship returning in ballast with bricks from some foreign port — probably the first bricks brought to this country. This business was discontinued when the vessel, with an only and much loved son aboard, was lost in a storm.

Next to his own place, Mr. Fraser built the fine brick Georgian residence now occupied by Mr. H. M. Doull. It was built for his granddaughter, Augusta Isabella Henkell, who married Lieutenant George Robinson of the 60th Royal Rifles, stationed at Annapolis Royal. Dr. Henkell (staff surgeon to His Majesty's Forces) procured the plans for this house from the engineer at the fort. It was of the type standardized for married officers' quarters and erected in many different parts of the world, but this is the only example here. Today it would be difficult to make alterations as the outside walls are of eight-tier brick and the inside partitions of four-tier brick. Citizens point with pride to this house as it was the birthplace of "our good old doctor" — Dr. Augustus Robinson. His father, Lieutenant George Robinson (who retired at the age of 28), lived here with his family of six boys and six girls.

The late Dr. Robinson, as a family doctor, had a remarkable record of having practiced amongst us for 50 years, right up to the time of his death at 90. He will be remembered for his cheerful wit, his mental gifts, and his unflagging zeal in leaving no call unheeded. A tablet in the Town Hall, erected by his friends of the town and countryside, to the "beloved physician," tells its own story.

Birthplace of Dr. Robinson

One of the doctor's stories is as follows: "One evening as my mother was walking home, she felt something about her feet, and looking down she saw a little grizzled dog with a bushy tail. As she couldn't rid herself of him she took him home. She made inquiries and advertised, but could find no owner. He was named Gipsy and became her devoted companion. During her illness of seven weeks, the dog spent the whole time under her bed, and when she died, disappeared, never to be heard of again."

Colonel Frederic Davoue, a noted Loyalist, lived in a house near the Baptist Church long before our memories. Quoting from an article of Mrs. Owen's: "A mile from the fort lived the Davoues. Colonel Davoue, after the evacuation of New York, left his farm in New Rochelle and came to Annapolis Royal. The family were originally French and a great, great-granddaughter has a bit of the family china brought from France, and always kept it packed in straw except when needed to deck a feast. It is white with a gilt edge, decorated with mythological figures in red. Mr. Davoue "kept slavery" and brought with him the original Aesop Moses, the first of the long line bearing that name since then to be found in Annapolis Royal. Mr. Davoue's two daughters, Bathiah and Susannah, shared in the amusements of the town and, as their father was very particular with them, they were driven to and from the balls by old "Zip" as a precaution against possible beaux. What did that avail? The young men walked home with the ladies. Zip drove slowly. When he neared the house, he bundled his young mistresses into the coach and on arriving home he reassured Mr. Davoue with a cheery, "All right, massa." The girls in gratitude to this "shut-eyed sentry" compassed him with sweet observances in the shape of mittens, socks, and mufflers. Zip was eventually given his freedom, but such was his attachment to the family that he refused to take it.

In the southeast corner of the old Davoue property at the Mile-Board was the family cemetery, now quite obliterated, in which there were supposed to be about 30 persons buried: Davoues, de St. Croixs, Huguenots, and some slaves. When as a girl, Mrs. Maude W. Malcolm (great granddaughter of Colonel Devoue) was walking through this cemetery, she was attracted to an unusual headstone. Pulling away the moss to read the inscription, it was found to bear this strange epitaph:

> 18 years a maiden,
> 1 year a wife,
> 1 day a mother,
> Then I lost my life.

Mrs. Malcolm asked her mother the meaning and was told the following story: In those days men often proceeded to distant places and were absent often many months after much voyaging. So it seems a young husband returned after his journeying without having heard from his wife. He was met at the door by her mother who, without saying a word, led him across the field and through the gate to the little grave, pointing to this stone. He suddenly realized what it all meant and — whether this be legend or not — where he suddenly clapped his hands to his head in grief, his hair next morning was found to have turned white. He would not even see the child, but, leaving a suitable sum for its maintenance, he straightway left, never more to return.[5]

What is known to us as The Gables (built by James LeCain, great grandfather of Mr. James Horsfall) originated from a very old, small dwelling into the present up-to-date four-apartment house. It has had many owners, having large families. The first we know about was Mr. Grassie, a lawyer, with six girls and four boys. Another, for many years, was the Hon. J. B. Mills, M.P., who gave it the name of Oak Hill from the large oak trees on the adjoining hill. It was Mr. L. M. Fortier, who, coming here in 1913, gave it its present name. It occupies land on what is known in Captain John Knox's *Journals* (1757-1760) as Babinot's Hill. He tells us about a fort there on the southwestern extremity having "6 swivel guns, a sergeant, gunner, and 15 rank and file who mount guard there every day."

This large estate is being gradually parcelled off into building lots.

Mr. Laurence Munroe's house, as the home of Mr. Israel Ruggles, was one of the prettiest in town, with a beautiful

---

[5] The names used in this story as published hitherto are omitted, as they were subject to contradiction.

garden and lime trees that had been imported from England. Extending the length of the house upstairs was the ballroom, prettily decorated, while on each side were wings, which have since been removed, giving the place a modern appearance. Many servants were at the beck and call of the family, the children not being allowed to go to the kitchen even for a drink, but were required to order a servant to do the task. Here was lavish entertainment and there are tales of too much wine being imbibed, necessitating the removal of those afflicted. If this were so, we must in charity pass it over as a not uncommon occurrence in every garrison town. Later this was also the home of Colonel DeLancey Harris's family for many years.

The Binning house was built by Mr. Thomas Ritchie, cousin of Judge Ritchie. Though now renovated, that it is old is known from the log foundation. Mr. Forbes, the old Scotch schoolteacher, also lived here. With him, knowledge must be imparted if to the extent of cruelty. His wife, on her arrival in Annapolis Royal, is described as being bright and pretty and was dubbed "New Coinage" from the new coins of Queen Victoria's time, but he was an "Old Tartar." Forbes would say to his wife, "Margaret, I thirst," and she would immediately comply with a bottle. He said of her when dead that she made him a faithful servant.

It is a long road that has no turning, and now we have come to it. These fragmentary bits — faint glories of the past — gathered at this late date in the history of Annapolis Royal make us realize that much more important and interesting data might have been preserved, when we recall the centre of authority and influence that the old town occupied from so early a date and for so long a time.

THE ROMAN CATHOLIC CHURCH
(ST. THOMAS'S)

Churches have come and gone since Lescarbot gave religious instruction in "the little chapell built after the savage fashion," since D'Aulnay Charnisay built a church[6] and college for the Capuchin monks sent out from France by Cardinal Richelieu in 1632.

Parkman gives us a wonderfully vivid description of the first Christian baptism in North America: "Old Membertou was first catechized, confessed his sins and renounced the devil, whom we are told he had faithfully served during 110 years. His squaws, his children, his grandchildren, his entire clan were next won over. It was in June, St. John Baptist's day, when the proselytes, 21 in number, gathered on the shore at Port Royal. Membertou was named Henri; his principal squaw Marie (for the Queen); one son after the Pope, another for the Dauphin; his daughter Marguerite after the divorced M. de Valois; and in like manner the rest of the squalid company exchanged their barbaric appellations for the names of Princes, nobles and ladies of rank. Membertou was for war on all who would not turn Christian. Fr. Biard taught him to say the Lord's Prayer. At the petition, 'Give us this day our daily bread,' Membertou remarked, 'but if I ask for nothing but bread I shall have no fish nor moose meat.'"

The tercentenary of this Baptism was commemorated in the present Roman Catholic Church by a brass tablet on the walls and the Stations of the Cross. The tablet reads: "This tablet and the Stations of the Cross in this Church

---

[6] This church was traced to the finding of two apostle spoons which were dug up on the farm of Mr. G. Hoyt, Lequille.

are erected a Memorial of the Baptism at Port Royal (now Annapolis Royal) on St. John the Baptist's Day, June 24th, 1610, of Henri Membertou, Chief of the Micmac Indians, and his family — the first fruits of the Catholic Missions and the beginning of Christianity in Canada, A.D. 1915. Ad Majorem Dei Gloriam."

The small fine paintings of the Stations are set in frames made by one of the Native Indians from apple-wood of early French planting. At this celebration Father Grace was assisted by the Indians, who performed their part of the ceremony with dignity and reverence.

Space will not allow the telling of Madam de Guercheville, the great French lady who gave such financial aid in supporting her religion, of the Jesuit Fathers, of Abbe Sigogne, and of that long list of missionaries and priests who worked so zealously in this field.

An outstanding figure of later years is that of Father Grace, parish priest, beloved for his saintly character by all classes and creeds. The present Roman Catholic Church was built mainly through his efforts. Here he lived through the greater part of his ministry and here he celebrated his Golden Jubilee when he was elevated to the rank of Monsignor. It was his wish that he be laid to rest in the cemetery under the shadow of the little old church (called St. Louis[7]), where he celebrated his first Mass just 57 years before. It was a unique and imposing cortege, with the Archbishop of Halifax and 32 priests in the procession that wended its way down the long St. George Street to carry out that wish.

[7] Church demolished in 1930.

One of the treasures of this church was a very interesting old missal, published in Paris in 1720 and used here before the expulsion of the Acadians. It was carried about by the priests as they went from place to place. It is now in the Archbishop's House in Halifax. Another is a small hand-carved altar, the first one brought out from France.

THE CHURCH OF ENGLAND CHURCH
(ST. LUKE'S)

St. Luke's Church

Taken from a pamphlet published by the writer in 1922.

The oldest record of this church in existence dates from 1784. In regard to the present building, there is this article: "It having been represented to His Excellency, Sir George Prevost, Bart., the Lt. Governor of Nova Scotia, His Excellency was pleased to forward the said representations to England and His Majesty having taken the same into consideration was graciously pleased to direct that the sum of £500 should be appropriated, and applied towards erecting a building and finishing a church in the said Parish provided the inhabitants thereof would make vigorous exertions on their part to raise a sum of money to effect this object." Also — "At a meeting of the Vestry of St. Luke's Church at six p.m. on Saturday the 9th February, 1811 — two petitions were drawn up, namely: one to His Excellency, His Majesty's Council, praying them to give limits to the Parish of Annapolis — the other to His Excellency, Sir George Prevost, praying him to intercede with His Majesty for a piece of ground from off the southwest corner of the field belonging to the Government called the White House[8] field, for a situation for the new church."

The Rev. Cyrus Perkins, who had succeeded the Rev. Jacob Bailey, was rector and also chaplain to the forces of His Majesty King George III from 1808 to 1817. It was during his incumbency that the first move was made to erect the present building. Rev. Cyrus Perkins was afterwards drowned while yachting in Tor Bay on one of his trips to England.

The old church on Church Street had been sold and Governor Lawrence had previously ordered the removal from Annapolis Royal of "all manner of utensils, now or formerly used for the celebration of Divine Service" and sent to Halifax, presumably for safekeeping. This included the Communion Set given by Queen Anne to the Church here at the time of the Conquest. Now in St. Paul's, Halifax, it is one of their greatest treasures. Other gifts of olden days include the big King George III Bible (1781) and two old Chippendale chairs given from a home set of the late Mrs. Brittain's.

---

[8] This field had formerly belonged to French owners and had been held in trust for fortifications, if necessary, but was bought by the Government in 1765. (See Calnek and Savary's *History*.)

It was not until 1826 that the Church was consecrated, the Bishop having been notified that it was completed at a cost of £1,400, the S.P.G. (Society for Propagation of the Gospel) making a grant of £400. Several years elapsed before the spire was erected. George Runciman gave £50 towards its completion. The present bell, a gift of Judge Ritchie, has on it in raised letters "Quondam tu solus sanctus. Tu solus Dominus" (Thou only art holy. Thou only art the Lord). A letter written at this time says: "The new bell has arrived and may it be heard from General's Bridge to Land's End in calling the people to prayer." It was rung at 9 a.m. for soldiers' service, at 10 a.m. for the Sunday school and again at 11 a.m. for the people's service. This custom is still retained although no garrison is here to heed the 9 a.m. call.

In the beginning the government had contributed £500 on the condition that pews should be reserved for the soldiers. Here sat some famous regiments, such as the "Fighting 40th," the Highlanders, and also soldiers who afterwards formed part of "the noble 600" immortalized in Tennyson's "Charge of the Light Brigade."

Rev. John Millidge, D.C.L. (1817-1830), was successor to Mr. Perkins. He died while administering Communion in the old church at Clementsport and was buried by his own request under the chancel of St. Luke's. The vestry on this occasion were ordered "to wear a crape on the arm two mos." The late Dr. Robinson used to tell this story: When the new chancel was built, two brown paper parcels, each containing a white frilled shirt marked "J.M." were found, one at each end of Dr Millidge's grave. The inference is that his old Irish servant put them there in readiness for the resurrection day.

The interior of the church was then quaint and attractive, having galleries and square boxed pews (36 in number). The "goodwill" or right of occupancy of these pews was auctioned off, then rented and rated from 40 to 50 shillings. Anyone failing to fulfill his obligations was posted on the door of the pews. The records say that one pew at the back was reserved for the use of strangers.

The pulpit was a three-decker, of the "wineglass" type. In the lowest part sat the vestry clerk. This position was occupied by lchabod Corbitt for nearly 50 years, and in that time he had missed only two Sundays on account of illness. It is related of him that in his last days, when his mind failed, he was often heard making up his Easter accounts, which were so minutely kept.

The church was first lighted by candles stuck in small tin holders or candelabra and snuffed by the sexton; later by lamps burning oil —before electricity came into use.

Lovers of antiquity deplore the loss of the quaint furnishings of the type peculiar to the church of that period — but Annapolis Royal was modern, and such was the vandalism, as we like to call it, of the Victorian era.

The rectorships of the Rev. Edwin Gilpin, called the "venerated rector" (1852-1860), the Rev. J. J. Ritchie (1860-1891) and the Rev. Henry How (1891-1917), occupied a space of 85 years. It was during the ministry of the last named that the bicentenary, commemorating the first Church of England service held in Canada, was held in 1910. Many distinguished clergy from various parts of Britain, the United States and Canada attended. The service was held that day on the site of St. Ann's Chapel in the fort grounds where the Rev. John Harrison had first held a service of Thanksgiving 200 years before following the capture of Port Royal from the French. At the request of Rev. How, His Majesty King George V sent a handsomely bound prayer book in the care of the bishop of London. It is 19 by 21 inches, is bound in red leather set with amethysts, and has a Celtic cross of gilt on its cover. On the flyleaf is written: "For the Church of Annapolis Royal, Nova Scotia, on the occasion of the Bicentenary commemoration, September, 1910. From George R. I."

Modern memorials in the church of today include stained glass windows to the memory of the Gilpins and the Robert Harris and D. P. Harris families. Both the Harrises were natives of Annapolis Royal. Here it was that the former Chief Justice Harris was baptized, confirmed, married, and was given the last rites at his funeral service when he died in 1931.

The old church records contain some interesting and amusing entries such as:

> 1828 — 1 pt. spirits to persons assisting in putting up and taking down stoves.
>
> padlock for gates.
>
> for a whisk broom — the other having been broken by Rose (Fortune).

From the Rev. Jacob Bailey's memoirs, we learn of the glebe lands belonging to St. Luke's. They ranged from 500 to 288 acres in extent and rented from £6 to £27 annually.

METHODIST CHURCH
NOW UNITED CHURCH OF CANADA
(ST. GEORGE'S)

Calnek and Savary's *History* tells us that "in July, 1782, the Rev. William Black, the silver-tongued orator of early Methodism in the Maritime Provinces, visited the county and preached with fervour and effect at Annapolis Royal."

A large meeting house was built in 1793 after the Puritan manner in the style of the Barrington Church, which still stands. The old church stood on the corner of Church and St. Anthony streets.

We glean a little information of this church's history through its record as entered by the circuit steward, Mr. Andrew Henderson. "Deacon" Henderson, ever a champion of the Wesleyan cause, left many descendants in the Andrew Hardwick family who have always zealously upheld its principles.

The earliest entry in the records is dated 1834 and reads: "At an appointed time the committee for purchasing ground on which to erect a mission house met in the chapel in Annapolis Royal and as it was thought impracticable to carry the above plan into execution, it was thought advisable to petition the committee in London to use their influence at the Ordnance Department for liberty to occupy an acre of Government land in Annapolis Royal." Further entries in the records: "It was unanimously decided that the sale of the parsonage premises, namely — house, yard and garden — to the Misses Harris for £55 and the land to Arthur Ruggles for £75 be confirmed, and also the purchase of the Ritchie house and premises in Annapolis Royal for the sum of £175, confirmed 1863."

"The premises were purchased and entered upon the 1st day of May last. After certain repairs were made — the balance remaining from the proceeds of Bazaar was paid to Mr. Cutler on receipt of deed, say £50, leaving the sum now due to the executive and executors of the estate £133" (1864).

From an old photo of the Lower Town, the new Methodist church known as St. George's, built in 1846, is shown as standing to the north of Mrs. S. O'Dell's property. This church, like St. Luke's, had its quaint interior furnishings too, such as box pews, etc., which were afterwards changed. It was moved via the town marsh in 1867 to where the United Church of Canada parsonage now stands. (The Ritchie house referred to, belonging to Judge Ritchie, stood on the corner where the St. George's is now and was removed to Victoria Street. It is the home of Mrs. George Rice, having undergone many alterations.)

Again, there were changes, for under the energetic leadership of Rev. I. Porter-Shirley, the church of 1846 was torn down, the parsonage put in its place, and the large commodious brick building as we see it today in the United Church of Canada, built on the corner. The laying of its cornerstone was attended by much ceremony. The stone next to the parsonage is interesting; having been used in three places, it bears the following inscription:

W. Black, 1798 Relaid 1911.

Another has:

St. George's Church
First Church built A.D. 1798
Second Church built A.D. 1846
Third Church built A.D. 1911

Thus it will be seen that three churches marked the rise of Methodism in Annapolis Royal in a period of 154 years.

PRESBYTERIAN CHURCH
(ST. ANDREW'S)

There seem to be no records preserved of the early Presbyterian Church. The first Presbyterian congregation was organized in 1855, the promoters being George Runciman, a native of Scotland, James Gray and Arthur King. A church was built in 1862 which was afterwards altered and enlarged under the ministry of Rev. Bruce Muir, a native of Scotland.

The church, though never having a large following, is remembered for its many able preachers. It united with the Methodist in 1919. The building itself has since been made into the residence of Mrs. S. M. Brown and Miss Agnes Munro.

BAPTIST CHURCH

Records of the Baptist Church having been destroyed by fire, there is a dearth of material. The following extracts, from old letters and reminiscences, have been taken from an article prepared for its Jubilee Anniversary Service, Sunday, September 7th, 1924, by the pastor of that time, Rev. A. Gibson, and are published by his kind permission:

"Previous to 1873, the 'two or three' had met together in some home and occasional services were held in the Court House." In June, 1874, this item appeared: "The few Baptists in the old capital of Nova Scotia have already erected a beautiful house for the worship of God." More money was required to finish and to furnish it and arrangements were made for a Tea-Meeting and Bazaar to be held on July 1st. At the Jubilee exercises a lady told of the following incident: In preparing for this Tea-Meeting, she with her sister was sent, each one "to pick a Yankee pail of strawberries." When it is recalled that each of these pails held 12 quarts, the zeal of the workers becomes apparent.

From the *Christian Messenger*, September 9th, 1874, comes the following account of the Baptist organization: "On September 2nd the Baptist Church was organized in Annapolis Royal town with membership of thirty-four. The members present of this new church assented to the Articles and the Covenant of the Associated Baptists of this Province. Isaac Healy was then chosen as Deacon, Rev. T. A. Higgins as pastor." Mr. Higgins wrote of the organization: "The few Baptists in Annapolis Royal deserve great credit for erecting this good and comfortable edifice — the services of T. Whitman, Esq., deserve special notice for without him the work could not have been done." A debt of $400 remained, but in 15 minutes this amount was raised. A further $400 was yet required for the spire and some external items.

It was in December, 1874, that 13 candidates were received for Baptism. There was no convenient place and in the meeting someone suggested a baptistry in the Church. The idea seemed hazardous, as the building was just barely completed. However, the suggestion was received and in a few days the work was done. On this occasion Mr. Higgins wrote: "It was a day of peculiar interest to us as it was probably the first time the ordinance of baptism by immersion was observed in this town." Those present pronounced the occasion as "peculiarly solemn and impressive." Mr. Higgins also wrote of having secured a temporary parsonage and that friends who had dropped in unexpectedly had "after short intercourse, left $43.37."

The same year the pastor reported two very interesting Sunday schools — the one in Annapolis Royal being conducted by Br. J. L. Brittain. At the roll call on February 4th, 1898, the pastor recorded, "The energies of the year had been occupied in building a pastorium, by the providence of God one of the best in the Maritime Provinces." (That parsonage, built during the incumbency of Rev. J. G. Coulter-White, is now the home of Mr. J. McClafferty.)

Many up-to-date improvements have been made in the church and 23 pastors have been resident here during those 50 years.

Mr. Andrew Beardman Hardwick and his son, Rufus Hardwick, deserve special mention for their interest in the church's progress. Their gifts include the church bell in

1899, the pulpit and the Bible in 1873. There also were bequests by the will of the late Mr. Rufus Hardwick of $500 for a tablet to be placed in the church as a memorial to the Hardwick family and $500 for paying off the mortgage. Both were done at one ceremony.

Rev. N. A. Whitman, in 1904, remarks that "the Annapolis Royal pastorate was one of the most pleasant he ever had." The clerk, Mr. Frank Barteaux, wrote: "Fifty have united with the church and the majority by baptism. The field was never in such a prosperous condition."

Rev. A. Gibson concludes his compilation of the history of the Annapolis Royal Baptist Church thusly: "At the close of fifty years the church has many reasons to praise God. It is in good heart and a fine spirit prevails. For the future we can only say with the missionary, 'The prospects are bright as the promises of God.'"

The Diamond Jubilee of the Baptist Church was observed on Sunday, July 29th, 1934.

SCHOOLS[9]

Beneath the shelter of a log built shed
The country schoolhouse next erects its head,
No 'man severe' with learnings bright display
Here leads the opening blossoms into day:
No master here in every art refined
Through fields of science guides the aspiring mind,
But some poor wanderer of the human race
Unequal to the task, supplies his place;
Whose greatest source of knowledge or of skill
Consists in reading and in writing ill,
Whose effort can no higher merit claim
Then spreading Dilworth's great scholastic fame.

(From "The Rising Village" [Annapolis Royal] by Oliver Goldsmith, relative of the noted poet of that name, written in 1834.)

The following excerpts have been taken from an article, "Early Education in Nova Scotia," by Mr. P. N. Thibeau, M.A.:

"Education in Nova Scotia is of religious inception. Our pioneer schoolmasters were members of the Capuchin Order of Missionaries who came to Acadia with Governor Isaac de Razilley in the year 1632. Before the end of the next year, they opened a Seminary at Port Royal (Annapolis Royal) for the education of Indian children and converts. It is recognized to be the first school in Acadia. A far greater

---

[9] From a paper prepared by the writer for the Historical Association, 1924.

distinction than this is sometimes conferred on it by writers, who assert that it was the FIRST school to be opened on the whole continent of North America. Its establishment, it is said, antedated the pioneer schools of New England."

"The Capuchins came to Acadia as representatives of the sacred congregation for the Propagation of the Faith. A report on the state of this school which was submitted to headquarters at Rome in 1633 and preserved in the Archive of Propaganda shows that at this early date it was already on a prosperous footing. Attendance was even then good and the numerous conversions in the vicinity of the settlement indicate how beneficent was its influence and how successfully it was being used as an instrument to facilitate the indoctrination of the savages into the principles of Christianity. Upon the death of de Razilley in 1636, jurisdiction in Acadia was transferred to his associate D'Aulney de Charnisay. De Charnisay looked with favour upon the school; he had his daughters placed there for instruction and helped to make its cause prosperous. It also enjoyed the patronage of the great Cardinal Richelieu who provided for it a fair sustentation in the way of an endowment that was the chief source of revenue to the Capuchin missionaries in Acadia. Teachers were expelled after the death of de Charnisay, the school suffered from the long dissensions occasioned by the prolonged conflict of rival claimants for control in Acadia. In 1652 a French trader by name of La Borgne seized Port Royal and expelled the teachers of the Seminary. There were two of them, the Venerable Fr. Cosmo De Mentes and Fr. Gabriel de Joinville. The Directress was a lady by the name of Madam de Brice D'Auxerre to whom the Viceroy de Charnisay had given the guardianship of his daughters. Subsequently, the teachers returned and when the English Colonial Forces took the settlement in 1654, the Seminary was being conducted by the Rev'd. Fr. Leonard of Chartres, Superior, appointed by Fr. Yoo of Paris, and two brothers, Brother John of Troyes and Brother Francis Mary of Paris. Their church was burned by the invaders and with it, likely, the humble school. The teachers themselves were compelled to take refuge in Paris. Two years afterwards there were no representatives of the Capuchin Order in all Acadia. An appeal was made for their return, but the continued return of the English and their decisive capture of 1710 put an end eventually to whatever evanescent hopes they entertained of resuming their Collegiate work at Port Royal."

"The first English schools in Nova Scotia resembled the earlier French Schools in that they were essentially on religious foundation." Mr. Thibeau further tells us that the Society for the Propagation of the Gospel in Foreign Parts and the Lords of Trade entered into an agreement whereby in every township land should be set apart for the maintenance of a minister, a church, and a grammar school. As an inducement to teachers an additional hundred acres were promised. These teachers were to hold the licence of the Lord Bishop of London. The salary was £15 per annum with a special gratuity of £10 to those who embarked with the first settlers. In 1732, Paul Mascarene, governor at Annapolis Royal, was sent to Boston to make this known to prospective immigrants coming from the New England colonies. Lieutenant Amherst further elaborated these proposals in 1745 by suggesting that the land be laid out in townships, four miles square divided into 66 shares in each of which appropriation would be made for a schoolmaster.

Gradually the work of these schoolmasters assumed a broader scope and, in addition to the study of Scripture and rules in church attendance, instruction of a secular kind, such as reading, writing, and acquaintance with secular literature, came to be imparted.

In 1727, 17 years after Nova Scotia fell to Great Britain, a request was made of the Society to provide a Chaplain for the soldiers in the Garrison at Annapolis Royal; Annapolis Royal then being the seat of Government of the Province. The next year a clergyman named Richard Watts was sent from England to take charge of the field. He was in all probability the first duly ordained clergyman of the English church to come to Nova Scotia after the conquest and with his advent education in the province under British auspices began. Rev. Watts arrived at Annapolis Royal towards the close of the year 1727. Being a very earnest patron of education he requested the Society before leaving England that it should provide him with a fund to enable him to erect a school for the instruction of poor children in his incumbency. A yearly gratuity of £10 was voted him for this purpose and at Easter the following year he began to hold classes, using prayer books and tracts supplied him by the Society for study books in the School. Primitive as the school was it made good progress under Mr. Watts's energetic management. He reported to the Society soon after its inception that he had about 50 pupils coming to him for instruction. As a result, the allowance of £10 was doubled in 1731. Still this provision seems to have been insufficient to meet the demand, for in 1736 the teacher undertook to enlarge the classroom at his own expense. But soon after this he received a call to go to Bristol in New England, and when he left

Annapolis Royal to assume the duties of his new charge in 1738, the activities of his school were discontinued.

As early as 1781 a very efficient high school was opened by Mr. Benjamin Snow. We learn of this from a letter written by the Rev. Jacob Bailey, who arrived on the scene in 1782 and who wrote to the Society for the Propagation of the Gospel: "I would like to acquaint the Society that the school at Annapolis Royal has been supplied for the year past by Mr. Benjamin Snow who received his education from Dartmouth College and who was expelled from New England for his loyalty. This gentleman may be recommended for his learning, sobriety and good morals to the Society's favour. He gives universal satisfaction to the people and is greatly beloved by the children whom with my assistance he catechises three times a week. We humbly request that the Society would admit him for their School master and allow him to draw for the usual salary." A further extract reads: "The Society has appointed Mr. Benjamin Snow their school master at Annapolis Royal with the usual salary of £10 commencing on Michaelmas last."

The Rev. Jacob Bailey, who was a graduate of Harvard and a writer of books, journals, and sermons, master of Latin and Greek, for his loyalty endured great persecution. He taught school here in Annapolis Royal and in connection with the work of St. Luke's Church, of which he was rector, he assisted in catechizing the young and visiting the schools. From his journal we read: "At Annapolis Royal I performed Divine Service on Wednesday and catechised nearly 80 children." "In 1785 regular schools are supported at Annapolis Royal where constant attendance is given for their improvement."

Our spelling "bees" probably originated from him for we read further: "I train my scholars in military exercises. I propose to set apart every Friday for Spelling and to appoint the boy who remains uppermost after the last word in the appropriated portion, captain, and the other officers successively in order." In his time schools were either male or female, and letters to the latter scholars are preserved showing how he lent them suitable books to improve their minds and his conversation with them being of a high order. "The female school conducted by his daughter in 1806 consists of thirty-four scholars, thirteen of whom are dependent upon charity. They attend catechising on Wednesday." In 1787, Mr. John McNamara succeeded Mr. Snow. Up to this time school teaching as a general thing had not been a distinct profession. Mr. Bailey says of him in 1787: "This school master is another extraordinary genius. He was born at Kennebeck, Maine, and came to live with me about the beginning of the rebellion."

For many years, "John" (as he was familiarly called) was a member of Mr. Bailey's family. He was first taken in as a servant. But during the compulsory absences of his employer in the last few years of his residence in Kennebeck, this young man was of essential service to the family and doubtless, on more than one occasion, prevented their suffering from want of the necessaries of life. Abandoning his native land with Mr. and Mrs. Bailey, he was of no little assistance to them after their arrival in Nova Scotia. This, Mr. Bailey states in his letter. That he who had been received into the family in such a subordinate situation should have had the force of mind to rise above the condition of a mere "hewer of wood and drawer of water," and availing himself of the opportunities which Mr. Bailey afforded him should have acquired the amount and variety of information which his employer says he possessed, shows that he could have been no common man. This, with the goodness of heart which characterized him, is enough to justify the humble effort now made to rescue his memory from oblivion. The high-born and wealthy have no lack of eulogists, while many who do not possess these advantages, although more worthy of praise, are forgotten. Another reference reads: "John McNamara has been fined £20 and imprisoned five days but now dismissed on bail." Bishop Inglis said in a letter to Mr. Bailey: "I very sincerely regret the death of Mr. McNamara. In him the community has sustained a very considerable loss."

From the extract given below we may surmise that his school was always under the supervision of the Rev. Jacob Bailey.

Annapolis Royal, December 12, 1784.

To the Reverend Samuel Peters,

Pimlico, near London, Great Britain.

I have enclosed you a bill drawn by Mr. McNamara our worthy schoolmaster on the Society — he is a young fellow brought up in my family and who endured with me not only persecution but imprisonment for his loyalty and if you would be kind enough to procure the enclosed articles you will greatly oblige us.

Invoice of articles mentioned in the above letter —

A pair of globes 12 inches in diameter not exceeding six guineas.

Stane's works, small octave.

Sheridan's Dictionary.

The Governess by Miss Fielding.

Elements of Criticism by Lord Haines, 8th edition.

Potter's Mathematics.

Newbury's little book for children to amount of guinea.

 A microscope not exceeding half a guinea.

Ferguson's Astronomy.

Littleton's Dictionary English and Latin.

History of Louisiana, 2 vol. 12 mo.

From the foregoing letter we get a fair idea of what subjects were taught in 1784.

In collecting data for schools, the most prominent man who comes to mind is Mr. Ichabod Corbitt. He was born in 1780 and died in 1861. Having become lame from an injury received to his knee early in life, he took up school teaching at the age of 14 and continued in that profession until his death — nearly 60 years — having taught four generations. He kept a remarkable school in his time and was a great disciplinarian. Mr. and Mrs. Corbitt, with their family of 10, lived in the Cummings house at the foot of St. Anthony Street. One large room upstairs was reserved for the "seat of learning." In winter it was heated by a large iron box-like stove, four feet by two feet. It is further said that snow tracked into the hall never melted until spring came! The seats were made of deal planks having supports of fence poles. On them the pupils sat, bolt upright at crude desks. In the latter were inkwells of lead, both they and the ink being made by the master himself. His pupils were only required to furnish a New Testament, a Goldsmith's *History of England*, Findlay Murray's *Grammar*, and Dilworth's spelling book. Dilworth[10] was the great standard of all school books at that time. It contained the alphabet, spelling, reading, fables, poetry, maxims, questions and answers relating to Scripture history, a dash of grammar, and sundry other useful knowledge. One of his pupils remarked that he "began in Dilworth and graduated in Dilworth."

He taught writing with great care and even his pupils of six and seven years could show a well-written copybook. His method of teaching the young beginner is the ingenious handmade machine which is now the property of the Fort Anne Historical Museum. Mathematics was his forte, using the "rule of three" as the basis for all that work. Some readers will remember:

> Multiplication is vexation,
> Addition is as bad,
> The "Rule of Three" perplexes me,
> Fractions drive me mad.

Mental arithmetic sharpened the wits of his pupils, while his knowledge of navigation was widespread, attracting the sailors off the ships for lessons. School opened at 9 a.m. (time having been previously taken from the sundial in the garrison) with Bible reading and prayers. Then when the scholars were lined up for his inspection, the stentorian command rang out — "Toes out, chin in, breast full, heels

---

[10] Following one of the fires in the Corbitt house, a copy of Dilworth was found under the debris. It is now in Fort Anne Historical Museum.

together and eyes on the master." It has been said that they obeyed instructions.

The late Dr. Robinson used to tell us how they spelled. With classes lined up on the floor, they would begin in quite a merry-like way, thusly: a, h, *ah*; o, h, *oh*; q, u, a, *qua*; q, u, e, *que*; q, u, o, *quo*; and so on to the end. Any words, taking "rudimentary" for an example, were spelled out as follows: r, u, d, *rud*; i, I, *rudia*; m, e, n, t, *ment*; rudiment; a, r, y, *ary*; rudimentary. We remember hearing our parents spelling "Constantinople" — that was a fine tongue twister.

Mr. Corbitt received some assistance from the older girls, called monitresses, who used to teach the younger ones and in that way helping themselves to retain what they had learned. The younger ones were afterwards examined by Mr. Corbitt.

Recess, if any, was at rare intervals. At 12 o'clock there would be a cry from some ever-vigilant watcher who would remind him that it was time to quit: "Sun's to the mark, Sir." This meant that when the sun had reached a certain mark that had been rudely carved on the window ledge, it acted as a sundial. Again at 1 p.m., they assembled and at 4 p.m. were dismissed with prayers.

Payments were made quarterly — the rich paying sufficient to allow the poor to be taught gratuitously. Holidays were also rare. Saturday was a half holiday, which was chiefly spent in gathering quills from the geese for their master to make his pens, in getting the week's supply of wood or cutting switches. Think of boys collecting long willowy switches, in anticipation, of course, that when used they would be for the discomfort of some pupil — certainly not themselves! Another holiday was his birthday, on St. Patrick's Day. The girls and boys were always so pleased to hear of funerals, as Mr. Corbitt attended, he being vestry clerk of St. Luke's. So the monotony of lessons was sometimes varied.

Even in our day, a little daughter of the Principal came to inform the pupils that there would be no school that day, "Papa's sick." "Hurrah!" was the answer as they took up the cheer. It mattered not how ill the teacher might be. Many stories used to be told of these old school times, and it was a favourite amusement to sit around in some central place and tell them in turn. Here are two by Mrs. Owen: "One morning a little girl came into the school room and on being asked 'What are you crying for?' said, 'Because Nelson's dead.' 'He's no relation to you.' 'No, but I'm crying because father's crying.'" Even in this distance of time there is something inexpressibly touching in the thought of this unknown man sobbing over the death of a hero. That must have been in December, 1805, as the news of the Battle of Trafalgar brought by a gun brig did not reach Nova Scotia until two months after the engagement. The other story is of Sir Fenwick Williams returning to Annapolis Royal. He was met by Mr. Corbitt with this: "So you thrashed the Russians," to which Sir Fenwick replied, "And yes, sir, *you* thrashed me many a time."

We cannot help but recognize the trace of humour running through those old school days, but education was no joke — far from it! For, as mentioned before, the pupils were thoroughly drilled in all the knowledge of that time and what they learned *stuck*. This school sent forth many well-educated young men who held prominent positions in town and province.

GRAMMAR SCHOOLS

In 1811 an Act was passed by the Provincial Assembly to establish a Grammar School in Annapolis Royal and other places for which £100 per annum was granted, with an additional £50 when there were more than 30 pupils (Calnek and Savary's *History*). Rev. John Millidge, Rev. Cyrus Perkins, and Judge Thomas Ritchie were the first trustees of this Grammar School. In Haliburton's *History* there is this item: "March 29, 1826, £200 voted by the House as an annual vote to Academy at Annapolis Royal, twenty-four to four." And again: "This, together with the tuition money, enables the trustees to engage two masters to take charge of the institution. The building contained two distinct schools, one of which is devoted to classical education, the other to the elementary and higher branches that are commonly taught in English schools." One teacher sometimes received the grant from the great Church of England Society. The building stood on what was then the southern end of the White House field, and now occupied by a tenement house near the overhead Railway Bridge. On the introduction of the new school law in 1866, the building was sold and the main part of it (exclusive of the wings in which two junior departments were kept) formed for many years St. Luke's Sunday School house. A new building adapted to the new law took its place, known as the Annapolis Royal Academy. This law, with the introduction of the principle of compulsory assessment for the erection and support of schools, was unpopular. We read: "If Annapolis Royal does not pitch the school bill and the inventors of it where they ought to be — where good people don't go — then they deserve to be treated as they have been henceforth and forever."

From a speech of the Hon. Joseph Howe's in 1849 advocating free schools: "Take Annapolis — Ichabod Corbitt teaches fifty-one free scholars and draws £19; James N. Wheelock gets £14 and teaches only FOUR free; Richardson Harris draws £14 and teaches forty-two scholars eleven months; Bathia Robinson draws but £7 for teaching forty-seven a year; Henry J. Buxton gets £17:10s for teaching forty-four; while Jarvis Hartt gets but £14:15s for teaching ninety-one."

The schools were by this time graded; the elementary subjects and even a little Latin and French were taught in the "classical department." First licence issued in Nova Scotia was in 1759. Examinations were oral as well as written. Rev. Gilpin, a most interested patron, is one of those remembered who examined the pupils.

Some of the teachers of that first Academy are well remembered; remembered too, by those pupils on whom a deep and lasting impression was made. Like Ichabod Crane, "spare the rod and spoil the child" was a golden maxim ever faithfully borne out. It seems safe to say that the days of corporal punishment have passed, for "lickins" are now rarely known. Those were the days when for any misdemeanour or stupidity a dunce cap was put on the guilty one and he was made to stand in the corner, much to his own mortification. Another punishment was a placard put on the back of a pupil who was then made to walk up and down in front of the schoolhouse. It read, "Didn't know his lesson." It was said to be effective.

Mr. Charles Miller Forbes, a graduate of the University of Aberdeen, was headmaster of the Academy for 12 years after which he went into business and was later Registrar of

Probate until his death in 1883. He was a familiar figure on our streets, always garbed in a plaid shawl and many are the quaint stories told of him. His wife, who sometimes assisted him, adhered strictly to the principles of her husband, and they were both feared by the boys and girls alike. His manner of dismissal was unusual. At noon he stood with his back to the door, at which he would silently point, when there would be a general stampede; or again at 4 p.m., "We'll be giving up for the night, lads." Then prayer followed by a hearty "Amen" on the part of the pupils. (The exit would be a general slide down the banister and out of the door.) Mr. Augustus Fullerton, another teacher of the Academy, filled an honourable position in the cause of education in the town. He was, like his predecessor, an exacting and rigid disciplinarian. His scholars recall how they were compelled to commit to memory long paragraphs of history with not even a preposition omitted.

The late Mr. William Whitman of Brookline, Massachusetts, gives us some interesting bits concerning his education at this Academy:

"After being closed some months, the Academy was opened in the charge of Mr. Henry de Blois, who was a young man, a graduate of King's College and unmarried. I became a pupil immediately on the Academy's reopening. Mr. de Blois had rooms on Runciman's Corner, opposite the White House field. He had no assistants. As I remember, all the pupils were boys, varying from small to large. Reading, Writing and Arithmetic, but I think there was a Latin class for the larger boys. Annual examinations were held which included recitations, and I remember at one of these the boys played the Trial Scene from the Merchant of Venice. At another time I recited

Cato's Soliloquy and equipped myself for the part with a dagger borrowed from a veteran who had served under the Duke of Wellington at the Battle of Waterloo."

"The sanitary arrangements at the Academy were abominable and the grounds never had any care. Mr. de Blois was much interested in improving the grounds and was able to arouse interest in his scholars for this purpose. He, with his pupils, made frequent trips into the forest, selecting and uprooting suitable trees and transplanting them in the Academy's grounds. Although Mr. de Blois was at that time a young man only recently graduated from College, he preserved good order. Punishments were infrequent and never severe. One of the instruments of punishment was of his own manufacture, a well-planed, square wooden ferule about twenty-four inches long which he christened 'Dr. Birch.' Occasionally this was applied with the pupil lying across his knee, the master beating time to some popular song, the one that remains uppermost in my memory being 'The Campbells are Coming.' (This was during the period of the Indian Wars.) There was no water in the school premises and the boys brought it from a well in the Court House yard. Mr. de Blois gave up teaching early in 1853 and the Academy was closed. He later entered the ministry of the Church of England."

We may presume then that the big old oak tree which overhangs the railway bridge was planted by him (Mr. de Blois).

The former Superintendent of Education, Dr. A. H. McKay, taught here, also the late Chief Justice Harris — a native of Annapolis Royal.

How the memory harks back to those old school days. We can picture the scene — the pinafored girls with pigtails; the stout handmade shoes, all from the same last, which took a vigorous boy to make a start on them! or perhaps, in summer a good showing of bare feet; the slates accompanied by a small bottle of water with a rag brought from home. In this we are reminded of an expression of Sam Slick's: "Well, it rubbed all the writin' out of his face as quick as spittin' on a slate takes a sum out." There were the hard pine desks that made good whittling and bore the marks of the industry of former occupants — names of some who afterwards made their mark in the world. Also attention was paid to Bible reading, which in recent years has become optional. No less a person than Henry Ford said, "The way to get religious instruction is to get the Bible back into the schools. I think I got all the essence of the Bible in those days when I sat as a boy listening each morning to its reading. They developed a sense of right and wrong in us in those days."

This Academy became an annex to a fine hotel — the Dominion House — which was burned in 1887. The Grange was acquired in 1883, the history of which has been narrated. The trustees of the public school were singularly fortunate in being able to secure such a property which can boast of grounds unequalled in the Province. Prominent amongst the principals of this Academy was Mr. William MacVicar. We are indebted to him for his history of Annapolis Royal. The Grange building becoming dilapidated was removed, later torn down about 1900 and a new structure erected. This in turn fell prey to the flames, and was replaced by the up-to-date Academy of today.

Numerous private schools sprang up from time to time in different parts of the town, conducted by maiden ladies who were anxious to eke out a living from their scanty store of knowledge. They taught girls and small boys and usually in a room in their own home, where it would be convenient "to watch the pot boiling" at the same time. It was not considered necessary for girls to have too much education; if they mastered the "Three R's" and worked a sampler they were sufficiently finished scholars. Mrs. J. M. Owen says: "Every self-respecting child began the needlework of her life by executing a sampler." Bathiah Davoue's sampler was done on canvas in what is technically known as cross-stitch. There was a stiff border of impossible strawberries. First came the alphabet and some figures, then another row of the same absurd fruit, dividing the commonplace letters from the glory of this announcement, "Bathiah Ann Davoue, Her work, aged 8 years, Annapolis, May 14, 1803."

The task concluded with the moral sentiment and pious desire —

> Talk not wish not to appear
> More beauteous rich or gay
> Lord make me wiser every year.

In one of Colonel Mascarene's letters, dated July 20th, 1740, he writes to his agent, Mr. Douglas in Boston, that "Mr. Winniett is to carry two of Lt. Gov. Cosby's daughters to board at his own home in Boston." These young ladies were probably being taken to Boston for the benefit of the schools there, as were also his (Paul Mascarene's) own daughters. An article of Mrs. Owen's reads: "The young ladies of Annapolis Royal were sent to Miss Cunningham's select school at Windsor, where they were instructed in all that constituted a polite education and underwent the usual tortures of back boards and dumb bells —"

Here are the personal recollections of Mrs. A. D. Smith, daughter of the late Andrew Henderson: "There was an interesting school in Annapolis Royal which I attended long ago. It was kept by a Miss Maria Lovett. Her father had a small store near what we knew as the Foster House. He lived in a house close to the Haliburton House, afterwards Cowling's, and that is where the school was held. Nearly all the Annapolis Royal girls attended Miss Maria's school, where they were taught the usual lessons of a town school of those days. It was quite the thing for the girls, in turn, to go downstairs where her sister, Miss Elizabeth, instructed them in sewing, knitting and fancy work, including the making of samplers, so much prized in those days."

Another old pupil of that school said it was exclusive, limited to 12 pupils, and charged $3 a quarter. On being asked what she learned, she replied, "We were taught to be genteel." Lessons were from 10 a.m. to 2 p.m., and while in school they addressed each other as Miss so-and-so. On dismissal they heard, "You may retire," and then with a curtsey they backed down to the door. A girl had been known to have been called back as many as six times in order to teach her to leave the room properly!

At Miss Week's school, the paramount teaching seems to have been the Creed, the Lord's Prayer, and the Ten Commandments.

Then there was Miss Hepper, an English lady, who had a school for "higher" education and had French in her curriculum. Themes were a pet subject with her and one of them was remembered as "Ambition without a Talent." We wonder what the young pupil could do with that today.

Miss Patty Saunders, who lived in the Winniett house, gave many youngsters their start in education and is quite well remembered. The Misses Saunders also taught in the Officers' Quarters.

Another personal school recollection is that of Judge George A. Henderson: "My own recollection of school life begins with a Mrs. Robinson, who taught in the 'old meeting house,' the first building occupied by the Methodists, at the foot of the hill on the road leading to the Islands (for there were two islands in those days). Of course, my instruction was in the Primer and making of pot hooks, etc. She was a benevolent looking and kindly old dame, whose husband, John Robinson, taught out in the Perotte Settlement. Mrs. Robinson always had a thimble on her finger and her means of punishment was in tapping with a good deal of force her thimble on the children's heads. That handed out to me seems to have been a life punishment, for after the lapse of more than sixty years I can still feel it."

"Deacon" Henderson's Residence And Dormitory

ALBION VALE ACADEMY

The writer is indebted to Judge G. A. Henderson of Saint John, for the information concerning Albion Vale Academy.

Few realize, and fewer remember, that the old house (within recent years destroyed by fire) that stood on the Goucher place, now the Hillsdale Golf Course, was a private boarding school for boys, kept by Mr. Andrew Henderson. It was a fine property, having fruits and vegetables in abundance and showing signs of former French industry. He purchased this house and 150 acres of land and built his academy a little to the east of it, connecting the two with a rustic footwalk over the swampy land that intervened. Around the wall outside and in large letters was "Albion Vale Academy, 1837" while inside was "Thou God seest me." He considered it all pleasantly and advantageously situated and where the boys would be kept from bad associations and called it Albion Vale.

While teaching at Annapolis Royal the allowance of £35 annually for the combined grammar and common school was awarded to him by the commissioners, and in addition to that sum he was granted by the House of Assembly £100 in the new situation, and then £50 annually for many years. This was munificence unprecedented in the history of any English teacher in Nova Scotia. The Hon. Joseph Howe and Sir William Young were both personal friends and each was very much interested in the Albion Vale school. At one time he had 21 boarder pupils, coming from distant parts such as Bermuda, Saint John, and Halifax. Some of them were schoolteachers desiring of becoming more efficient, others became prominent in mercantile affairs and others masters of great ships.

Himself a strong pillar of Methodism in the country, he gave many a prominent Methodist, lay and clerical, a sound preparatory training. Besides his boarders, he had constant attendance of upwards of 30 day scholars. His teaching included the entire subject of arithmetic and bookkeeping by double and single entry. In addition to these branches were Geography, English Grammar, Plain Trigonometry, Navigation, and Algebra. I might add "Buck-Saw" to this curriculum, or do I mean "Gymnasium?" The Buck-saw was more practical in serving the double purpose of giving exercise and keeping the many big woodboxes filled, which each boy took his turn in supplying.

At this time Mr. Henderson had eight children who, with his servants and boarders, all lived in the old house (it then contained 15 rooms) which must have been taxed to capacity. This Academy was a great boon to the whole countryside, for we must remember that many of the inhabitants were of educated parentage who had come over during the American Revolution. Girls went as day pupils.

The secret of Mr. Henderson's success lay in the directing of the studies of his pupils into a course that he judged might be useful to them when they should engage in the serious affairs of life. He was a self-taught man, holding no degree from any college, but more than that, he was a born mind trainer. His scholars were taught to cultivate their memory and to observe. The result was that everything so absorbed remained permanently.

In regard to the Albion Vale school there is a ghost story, but the details are rather vague: It is about a man coming down the stairs of the house with his head in under his arm!

Copybooks of that school have been preserved in those of the late Mrs. Corey O'Dell and the late Mr. Bonnett Harris, brother and sister. Written when they were about 14 years of age, they are models of neatness and accuracy. As they bear the dates August 6th, 11th, etc., we are given to understand that vacations were omitted. The brother's copybook suggests the work of a skilled draftsman. Think of such a fellow being "apprenticed out" when a civil engineer's course would have been more to his liking! But there was no alternative. Any such course was not taught in that Academy or hardly thought of in these parts at that time.

The following letter (taken from the *Christian Reporter* and *Temperance Advocate*) is interesting:

> Albion Academy,
> Near Annapolis Royal.
>
> The public are respectfully informed that the above institution still continues in operation and open for the reception of pupils. No pains have been spared to render the situation pleasant and agreeable, as well as to make comfortable the circumstances of its inmates. All the branches necessary to form a good English, Mathematical and Commercial Education are here taught; nor are the moral or religious duties neglected. To these as by far the most important a considerable share of attention is directed and it is to be hoped a judicious mode of moral discipline, long and perseveringly pursued, has not been altogether in vain. Owing to a handsome grant from the Legislature the former very moderate rate of Board and Tuition is continued, viz: £25 per annum, each pupil bringing his own bed, bedding and towels, but no deduction for visits or vacations.
>
> ANDREW HENDERSON, Teacher of the Combined Grammar and Common School at Albion Vale. June 2, 1838.

ST. ANDREW'S SCHOOL

Many years had passed since "Deacon" Henderson's day, when again another private and day school for boys was opened in the Ritchie House, now the Queen Hotel. It was managed by Mr. H. M. Bradford, M.A., Cambridge University. A few girls as day pupils and some in residence at the Hillsdale also attended. Pupils were prepared and matriculated for the colleges McGill, King's, Kingston and others. This school was small, never having more than 25 pupils. It was an ideal place for such a school with its healthy situation, large grounds and gymnasium, and the town itself offering the advantages of the old Fort, the rink and the golf course. Boys came from different parts of Canada and several from the United States. Mr. Bradford's pupils had been very successful and his school a great acquisition. Being held in high esteem by everyone, it was much deplored when he decided to give up his teaching here in 1906 and removed to Halifax.

THE OLD MILITARY CEMETERY[11]

I like that ancient Saxon phrase which calls the burial ground "God's acre."

Rambling through the old military cemetery adjoining Fort Anne, we find much that is interesting. It is one of the oldest in North America, only an acre in area, but where there are supposed to be not less than 2,000 buried.

We are used to hearing of crosses on Flanders fields, but an old aunt of the writer's used to say that when on her way to school she saw the crosses there stand as thick as the fingers on her hand. More than a century has gone since that old lady passed that way. These crosses, together with the wooden slabs, soon fell under the ravages of time and now no record remains of them.

Most of the old existing monuments are of slate and freestone, having for design the cherub or skull head with wings and irregular printing and misspelled words. Intended to impress with reverence, they more often strike us as being grotesque.

There are 13 stones previous to 1800; one bearing the date 1720 is as far as can be ascertained the oldest in Canada. It reads:

> Here lyes ye body of
> Bathiah Douglass, who
> departed this life Octor
> the 1st, 1720, in the 37
> Year of her age.

---

[11] Taken in part from an article read by the writer before the Historical Association in 1920.

By the side of this is another stone (1740). Both are in good preservation and marking the graves of the wives of Samuel Douglas. There were two brothers, Alexander and Samuel Douglas, garrison officials presumably of Scottish descent, who had come to Annapolis Royal at the time of its conquest in 1710.

The second oldest stone is to Margaret Winniett. It is a singular fact that the tombstone to this child is the only one to that once prominent family. One looks the second time to see if one has read correctly. Yes, it says quite plainly that she was "born in 1723 and dyed in 1722." Evidently the engraver's mistake was allowed to stand for all time.[12]*

The large and recumbent and table-top stones are interesting. Those to the Gilpins have on them a crest of a boar sable armed, with the motto: "Dictus Factisque Simplex" (Simple in word and deed). Here lies Rev. Edwin Gilpin, formerly rector of St. Luke's and last garrison chaplain. He was a descendant of Rev. Bernard Gilpin, known as the "Northern Apostle" and father of the late Very Rev. Dean Gilpin of Halifax. (Richard de Gylpin in 1206 did service to his country by killing a wild boar which caused great damage to the adjoining mountain, and for this deed was awarded the Manor of Kentmere in Westmoreland, England, which has been in possession of the family ever since.) Several of these recumbent stones are to the memory of the Ritchies. One, to Judge Ritchie's wife sets forth her beautiful character in 22 lines of verse as composed by her sister. Truly a contrast to the abbreviations of today.

---

[12] Ed. note: Another possible explanation has to do with the two calendars used at this time. By one reckoning she was born in one year; by the other, she died in the previous year.

House Of Laura Johnstone

Nearby is a monument to Mrs. Ritchie's sister-in-law, Laura Johnstone, a native of Jamaica, British West Indies. The circumstances of her tragic death are related in *Recollections of a Georgia Loyalist* and can be told briefly as follows: Mrs. Johnstone, having held prayers with her household, two servants and a boy, retired to her room. Her baby having been put to bed, her last commands attended to, and the maid withdrawing. The maid had scarcely seated herself when she heard two knocks on the wall and hastening to Mrs. Johnstone, found her in flames. Another servant rushed in with a bucket of water, which was dashed over her, but it was too late, for she was burned fearfully. It is thought that she went to snuff her candle when the flounce of her muslin dress, put on for the evening, became ignited. Hers was a strong nature in matters concerning her spiritual welfare, but in temporal things she was apt to lean on others, having never been trained to think and act for herself, always depending on a governess, a parent or a husband. Had it been otherwise she might have shown some resource in putting out the flames; instead, she became confused over the danger of setting fire to the merino curtains of her bedstead to the risk of her baby's life. Thus on April 2nd, 1830, she sank into a stupor and her pure and gentle spirit departed this life. Her husband, who had been attending the House of Assembly in Halifax, was on his way home, making all haste possible. It being the last of March, however, the roads were bad for the journey by stagecoach, and in spite of travelling day and night, he reached Annapolis Royal only in time for the funeral. The baby was later to become the wife of the Rev. Rupert Cochrane and was to live in England.

Another stone of interest is that to the memory of Thomas Williams, commissary and barrack master (1778), his wife Ann Amherst (1778) and his son Thomas (1806). The son held the same appointment as his father in His Majesty's government. This family represent the grandfather, grandmother, and father of General Sir Fenwick Williams, the hero of Kars.

Some quaint epitaphs are to children. A daughter of Phineas Lovitt, MP, five months and four days (1812) reads:

> This lovely infant in full bloom
> Whom wishes could not save,
> Submitted to an early doom
> And sunk into the Grave.

One alluding to a son of Michael and Mary Spurr (1804) reads:

> The voice of this alarming scene
> May every heart obey
> Nor be the heavenly warning vain
> That called our friend away.

Another reads:

> Here lies the Body of
> Mr. William Rodda, Son of
> Mr. Stephen and Mrs. Theodisha Rodda,
> who Departed this Life
> July the 16th, 1763
> Aged 11 years and 9 Mo. —

One to an infant records that he was the "only" son of Mr. and Mrs. —, but adds that, afterwards, there were six more sons. Still another stone for a child aged six months shows much sentiment. The top carries the inscription "Early Transplanted" and underneath appears an engraving of a rosebud broken at the stem.

Homemade poetry is much in evidence:

> He liv'd Respected
> and Died Lamented.

Another epitaph reads as follows:

> In life esteem'd in death deplor'd
> The mouldering body lies
> Till the new Heaven and Earth restor'd
> Shall raise him to the skies.
> I hope my dear thou art at rest
> With saints and angels who are blest
> And in short time I hope to be
> In paridice along with thee.

These last verses were to Mrs. Beardman (1805) buried by the side of her husband. His, too, has poetry which says "he departed this life on munday the 6th of Sep. eight minutes before eight in the evening. In the year of our Lord 1819 in the 67 year of his age."

The iron fence fronting St. George Street was placed there by money in the amount of £100, bequeathed by the daughter of the Beardmans.

The following are examples of military epitaphs:

> Deposited here
> until the sound of the last trumpet
> the remains
> of Charles Alexander Simpson
> Assist. Surgeon 60th Regt.
> A native of North Medley, Staffordshire England
> He obeyed the mighty word Return.
> After an illness of 3 days
> in the 30th year of his age
> March 20th 1820.

SACRED

to

the memory of
ENSIGN GEORGE AUDLEY
of the Royal Newfoundland Regiment[13]
who died the 25th day of May 1806
in the 30th year of his age.

The remains of many others who had some standing in the military or civic life of the town are lying here, including those of George Henkell (1808), surgeon to His Majesty's Forces; Henry Watkys (1853), armour-bearer to His Royal Highness the Duke of Kent; Ichabod Corbitt (1861); Judge Thomas Ritchie (1852); Joseph Norman (1816), barrack master and ordnance keeper. Joseph Norman's wife's grave is marked by broken stone preserved in cement.

A modern stone to Rev. Jacob Bailey (1808) and Mrs. Bailey reads:

Frontier Missionary
First rector of this Parish
Which he served faithfully 28 years.

There were erected at the time of the Bicentenary of the Church of England in 1910 a stone and slab to the memory of Rev. Thomas Wood by the side of his wife's. Mrs. Wood's memorial is inscribed with quaint lettering. Mr. Wood's was unveiled by Judge Savary, through whose efforts the memorial was placed. Rev. Thomas Wood, a native of New Jersey, was both physician and surgeon and ministered in English,

---

[13] No longer in existence.

French, German, and Mi'kmaq. It has been said of him that as one of the S.P.G. missionaries, "few are deserving of greater honour than he." A pretty incident over his grave was when the late Bishop of London, who was present, said in his gracious and pleasing way, "I place here these flowers given to me by the children of Grand Pre on the grave of him who was the children's friend of his day."

Many an unknown person and many a romance lie hidden in this sacred acre. Headstones were not easily obtainable. Only a few lots show any affectionate regard for the reason that there are few representatives of the old families left. The cemetery adjoins the National Historic Park of Fort Anne, and while it is not under the jurisdiction of the Canadian Government, arrangements have been made to preserve its appearance and avoid the neglect that is unhappily noticeable in most old cemeteries.

THE NEGRO POPULATION OF THE COUNTY OF ANNAPOLIS

Taken from a paper prepared and read by
Frederick Wheelock Harris, November 11th, 1920.

When any person contemplates writing a history in connection with people belonging to the Negro race, the sources of knowledge or reference that may be consulted are, comparatively speaking, meagre. They are dealing with a race of people who, through unfortunate ignorance, were not able to produce persons of sufficient education or persons who took sufficient interest to chronicle events which took place in connection with their race or country as they occurred or as they were handed down to them. The records of their past, as far as they were chronicled by themselves, are unwritten; their history, if it could he called such, consists of information of various kinds passed on, one to the other, by word of mouth, distorted often-times by ignorance, imagination, superstition and not at all accurate.

So, to read the past of this branch of the human race, we have to consult records that have been written by those belonging to the white or Caucasian race who have taken interest enough in their less fortunate brothers in passing through life to make mention of them or to study their mode of life and habits.

It does not need mentioning that the Negro race essentially belonged to the continent of Africa, the popular belief being that these people are descended from Ham, one of the sons of Noah.

The Negro race now living on this side of the Atlantic, we regretfully have to say, came not to the continent of North America as bold adventurers of discovery, seeking new lands, homes or riches, but from ancestors torn from their homes in Africa by ruthless captors, thrust into the holds of foul ships, transported in chains thousands of miles from the place of their birth, after a voyage of exquisite suffering and torture at the hands of cruel and cunning men and accompanied by all the indescribable horrors that the detestable and damnable slave traffic implied. Such as survived the voyage were landed on the inhospitable shores of North America and the West Indies and sold like cattle or other beasts of burden to hard-hearted and cruel taskmasters. As the years went by, many changes took place. The descendants of some of these transported Negroes found themselves after a time in some of the New England States still, however, remaining in bondage to their masters. And from the New England States, they were brought into different parts of Canada.

By the last Dominion census, we are told that there were 5,747 Negroes in Nova Scotia. In the county of Annapolis, there were 515, Lequille boasting at that time of having 100.

We may accept it as a general rule that the progenitors of the Negro population of Nova Scotia were slaves. Slaves were brought into Nova Scotia at an early period of the history of the province.

In the census of the French in Acadia in 1686, there occurs at the end of the list of settlers at Cape Sable the name of "la libertie Ie neagre" or "liberty black." He was in all probability an escaped slave who had found his way thither from one of the English colonies. The prevalent impression that slaves were first introduced into this province by the

Loyalists in 1783-1785 has no foundation; in fact, whether they were first brought to the earliest English capital, Annapolis Royal, or to Canso, a port of much importance, is uncertain, as no records by the earliest Episcopal chaplains are to be found. About the first information or record of any kind that can be authenticated of a Negro in the county of Annapolis is found in one of the early Registry books at the Registry of Deeds at Bridgetown, in which may be found the conveyance of a mulatto girl, Louisa, sold in July, 1767, by Charles Proctor of Halifax, merchant, for £15 currency, to Mary Wood of Annapolis Royal, wife of Rev. Thomas Wood and assigned over to her daughter, Mrs. Mary Day, the year following.

According to the census returns of January 1st, 1771, seven Negroes were owned in the township of Annapolis Royal. Magdalene Winniett was the possessor of a man, woman, and girl; Joseph Winniett, of a woman and a boy; Ebenezer Messenger, of a man and Ann Williams, wife of Thos. Williams, of a man; John Stork, or Stark of Granville, was the owner of a man. Henry Evans of Annapolis Royal was the proprietor of a coloured girl. Henry Evans came from Sudbury, Massachusetts. He became a representative of the county. He was the author of the Evans journal as set forth in Judge Savary's history of the county.

Now this was previous to the great Loyalist inrush, which took place between the years 1783 and 1785. The still enslaved Negroes brought by the Loyalist owners to the Maritime provinces between these years, were classed as "servants" in some of the documents of the day. The word "slave" was more or less disliked by the British, so this alternative word "servant" seems to have been employed instead. Official lists show that with the Loyalists making permanent or temporary homes on the lower section of the fertile Annapolis Valley, came numerous slaves or servants, and that a goodly number also accompanied those exiles to whom were granted lands on or near the picturesque site of Digby. The names of the proprietors owning but one or two "servants" are too many for repetition. At Granville were Richard Betts, Charles Calhoune, Geo. Cornwall, J. T. de St. Croix, Abel Hardenbrook, and Thomas Robblee, each with three slaves, Ed Winslow with four, and Christopher Benson with six.

Among the slave holders of Annapolis Royal appear the names of Frederick Deveau, Andrew Ritchie, David Seabury, Lieutenant J. Reed, Abel Morrison, and Mrs. Kane, with three each; O'Sullivan Sutherland and John Totten, each with four; the Widow S. Grant and Geo. Sutherland, each with five; and Mrs. Chandler, with six servants. Fanciful names were bestowed upon the servants by their masters such as Cato, Pompey, Jupiter, Spruce, Aesop, and Sambo for the men; while we find names like Sukey, Sally, Sylla, Martha, Sary, Peggy, Phoebe, Nance, and Venus given to the women. In many of the records we find them referred to by one name and no surname. Later when slavery became a thing of the past, these servants or slaves adopted or appropriated the surnames of their masters. Hence, it is no surprise in the county to find Negroes bearing such names as Ruggles, Kane, Stephenson, Bailey, Johnson, Brown, Godfrey, Robinson, Fowler, Franklin, and Harris.

Generally speaking, the treatment given to this class of servants by their different masters while living in this county was of a generous nature and we have many instances recorded by means of last wills and testaments where proprietors of these Negro servants in bondage were not unmindful of their servitude to them and in a number of ways showed their appreciation. In the will of the late Frederick Deveau, who is mentioned above, the following paragraph appears: "I also authorize and direct my executrix and executor to execute and deliver to Aesop Moses, my late negro servant and his heirs and assigns the 100 acres of land in Clements from off lot number one which I intended to give him provided the said Aesop acknowledges to my said executor and executrix that he is sorry for his late conduct to me." Just what Aesop's grave offence was, I have not been able to learn, although I have made efforts to do so. However, it is gratifying to observe that he must have acknowledged to the said executrix and executor that he was sorry for his conduct as he appears later on the records of the county as the proprietor of the 100-acre lot referred to. Aesop Moses was one of the progenitors of the numerous members of the Negro Moses family with whom we are so familiar today in this locality.

I remember Aesop quite well myself when I was a small boy, and no doubt some of my hearers do also. Although crippled with rheumatism and bowed down with the weight of many years, the number of which he did not know himself, he jobbed around among the farmers at Lequille as long as he was able to do so. A resident grandson now bears his name, his cognomen, however, being shortened to Zip. Aesop Moses had a brother Henry. Henry in his day was to Lequille and vicinity what the Hungarian orchestra is now to the millionaire's home in New York. He supplied all the music needed for the dances of the day. The instrument upon which he was so proficient and from which he drew, or rather expelled, such harmonious sounds as to keep the lovers of the terpsichorean art on the floor until dawn, was nothing more or less than a pair of puckered lips through which he whistled all the popular airs of the day. It hardly needs mentioning that in order to keep his whistle in the high state of efficiency required by Henry's patrons, it had to be frequently wetted, so that no discords or ragged tones might result. Alas! If Henry were here today, what sort of music could be furnished with no wherewithal, so plentiful in the good old days gone by, to wet his whistle.

Rose Fortune

Contemporaneous with Aesop and Henry Moses, two notable characters dwelt in this town of Lequille, whom we can hardly pass by without some mention. One was Rose Fortune. Rose in her time held a monopoly of the trucking business, not through any letters patent, but by virtue of a strong right arm and strict attention to business. Her distinctive mode of dressing made her as much an easy mark to locate when needed as the tinkling bell of the truck men on the street today. She wore generally, I am told, a white cap with the strings tied under her chin, surmounted by a man's hat. She wore a man's coat, a short skirt, and high-legged boots. Armed with a good heavy wheelbarrow, Rose waited each day as the Saint John boat discharged her passengers and baggage at one of the wharves in the town, and no trunks or carpet bags, no matter how large or heavy, had any terrors for her; she handled them all with neatness and dispatch and transferred them to any part of the town for a modest charge. A picture of Rose, which is said to be a very good one, by those who remember her, holds a place of honour in the museum of Fort Anne.

Some of her descendants in the town today carry on a trucking business, supplying as did their ancestors a most satisfactory service to the public.

The other person I would like to mention is Ben Prince. He lived at Lequille, a most curious old character. His outward raiment was such that always called attention to himself; he had the dodging of any work to be done down to a science and spent most of his valuable time visiting around among the white residents of Lequille and vicinity. As part of his regular equipment, he always wore a tall glazed hat. His ideas, I would judge from what I have been told as to what was yours and what was his and what was other people's were sometimes distorted. My grandmother once related a story to me about old Ben that I thought rather amusing. He paid a visit one day to my great-grandmother, old Mrs. Easson. Coming into the kitchen, he found no one about. In front of the fireplace was a large pan of dough that had been just put down to rise. Old Ben took a look around to be sure that there was no one handy and then quickly filled his high glazed hat with the soft dough. Just then he heard Mrs. Easson coming, so he popped his hat, dough and all, on his head. Mrs. Easson rather suspected from Ben's confused manner that he had been up to something, especially as he made ready to go so quickly, so she constrained him to stay awhile and have a chat. He said he was afraid to remove his hat as he might catch cold. Very soon Mrs. Easson's suspicions were confirmed by the dough running down from under the hat across old Ben's face. He was then induced to remove his headpiece and, amid the roars of laughter from Mrs. Easson and other members of the family whom she had called into the kitchen at the comical sight of old Ben's woolly head covered with the soft white dough, he fled the scene.

The late Isaac Bonnett, in his will dated 1803, says: "My desire is that my black boys, George, Tom and Bob, be taught to read distinctly and write a legible hand, and that they be set at liberty as they severally arrive at the age of 24 years, each to be allowed a suit of good new clothes of every description, besides the common wearing apparel." He goes on to give the date of birth of each boy.

In the will of Ann Cosby, dated March 14th, 1788, of which Joseph Winniett, her brother, was an Executor and Thos. Williams another, both of whom we have before referred to, we read: "I also do give and devise unto my black woman Rose, a mulatto girl named Agatha and my black man named John Buckley, to each and every one of them their full freedom and discharge from all the servitude as slaves from the day of my decease forever." We can take it from the following story that Joseph Winniett was a kind-hearted man towards his servants. It is said that a slave girl had one day during Mr. Winniett's absence from home, provoked to the utmost the patience of her mistress. On his return Mrs. Winniett demanded a severe whipping for the slave at the hands of her master. Having ordered the girl to an adjoining room, Mr. Winniett charged her to scream at the top of her voice while he proceeded to apply his whip with such vigour to the furniture as to make everything rattle and then, at the opened door, the satisfied mistress informed the refractory girl that she had learned a lesson without any mistake this time!

In a great many instances, however, the proprietor of a slave or slaves bequeathed such to his heirs, and we have many records of such in our own Probate Court in this County.

David Randall, in his will dated 1785, makes the following bequests: "Item, I give Kezia my said wife, a red milch cow without horns and my black mare, and also the use of my negro wench, Sukey, during the life of my said wife, and after the death of my wife, I give my said negro wench to my said daughter Newcome and granddaughter Mary Shay to be by them sold, and the money arriving from the sale to be equally divided between them, share and share alike."

Joseph Totten, of the firm of Joseph Totten & Co., who did business in this town years ago, by his will dated 1788, to his wife Susannah, in addition to certain real estate, gave during her life the use of slaves, horses, cattle, stock, etc. He goes on to say: "I give and bequeath my negro slave girl, Clarinda, to my daughter Phoebe Totten, my negro slave girl Silvia, to my daughter Mary Totten, and I give my negro slave Bella to my daughter Jane." One cannot help but hope that each daughter was satisfied with the slave girl allotted to her. The Tottens at one time formed part of the Annapolis Royal "400" and Calnek and Savary's History says they were a highly respectable family. In the inventory of the estate appears the following item: one Negro £50; one Negro wench £60; three children £5. I take it that he was at all times prepared to defend his property and family honour as another item in the inventory is one case of pistols £5:6:8!

Crossing the river to Granville for a short time with our history we find the following records in connection with the early Negro residents. In the inventory of the will of Richard Betts, whom I have mentioned before, appear the following items: one Negro man named Toney £35; one Negro man named Primus £35; one Negro man named Harry £40; one Negro wench named Jane £35.

In the will of Jacob Troop of Granville, it is recorded as follows: "At the death of my beloved wife Anna, the black girl Hannah, if she served as a faithful servant till she is 30 years of age, she is to have her freedom but if she is not 30 years of age at the death of my beloved wife Anna, then her service is to be divided equally among my five daughters till she arrives at the age of 30, being now 11 years of age." Somehow when I read this extract from the will of Jacob Troop, my great sympathy went out to Hannah. I wish I could tell you how she made out. If it so happened that she had to be a faithful servant and please five different ladies until she was 30 years of age, she had indeed a hard path to travel. Let us hope she won her freedom.

There were more tender-hearted people living at Granville, however, as witness the paragraph from the will of

Joseph de St. Croix, dated 1814. I think we have mentioned this man before also: "And if my faithful servant Bess should choose to have her freedom, she shall be free and my sons shall pay her £10 a year during her life." I think I should have liked to work for St. Croix. It is quite likely that Bess stayed right on with the family.

George Cornwall of Granville, mentioned above, willed in I799 as follows: "I give to my wife Charity, all my negro slaves requesting her to manumit and set free by her will after decease, but in case they do not behave as honest or orderly servants, I wish that she should sell them as undeserving of her or my intended bounty towards them." We hope that the slaves, consisting of three men, lived up to their master's wish and dodged the threat at the end of the paragraph.

Caleb Fowler, of Granville, made a will in 1793 with somewhat similar provisions to Cornwall's referred to above. He bequeathed to his wife Mary, a Negro wench Hannah and her child Deana, so long as she remained a widow. The threat of selling a slave if he or she did not behave himself or herself had a salutary effect, as no doubt they would reason with themselves that if they were sold, they might run into a harder lot than the one they were already experiencing.

In 1786, Thos. Cornwall of Annapolis Royal, a reduced Captain in His Majesty late King's American regiment, gave to Isaac and David Bonnett, merchants of this place, a bill of sale of one farm, one Negro girl named Letisha, one roan horse named Beatable, one yoke of oxen, and some other articles. I looked through the inventory attached for the mate of the horse Beatable expecting to find one by the name of Hard to Beat, but Letisha, Beatable, and the oxen were the only livestock mentioned.

A story is told of one of these men in Granville, who used to run the ferry boat across the river semi-occasionally, probably doing even better than the present "John Hancock." The ferry boat was managed sometimes by a Negro servant, who was instructed to charge 6d. for each fare. A white man appeared one day on the Granville side, wanting to cross to Annapolis Royal. He said, however, he had no money. "But boss, all it costs is 6d.," says the ferryman in charge. "I know," says the man, "but I haven't got sixpence." The ferryman was in a quandary for a moment as he didn't want to disobey orders. Finally he said, "I tell you what, boss, a man that ain't got sixpence is jess as well off on dis side of the river as he is over in Annapolis Royal."

A conveyance was found not so many years ago in the cellar of the late Peter Bonnett, once High Sheriff of the county, dated in 1804, from Isaac Bonnett and other administrators of the estate of Robert Dickson, late of Annapolis Royal, to Wilbur Robinson and his heirs, of "a certain negro girl slave named Priscilla, about 8 years and 4 months of age, being part of the personal estate of the late Robert Dickson" and after the usual forms guarantees to the purchaser the right to the possession and services of the slave.

These Negroes, I regret to chronicle, did not always live in a contented manner with their masters. About this period, we find in different parts of the province, advertisements appearing in the newspapers of the time, offering rewards for runaway servants or slaves. Newspapers were not published in this Town at this early date, so I am not able to give any examples that refer to this particular locality except one from Digby appearing in the Royal Gazette, published in Halifax: "Digby, 21st June, 1792, run away Joseph O'Dell and Peter Laurence from their masters. £10 is offered as reward and all reasonable charges paid."

Of course, there were numerous advertisements about this period principally in the Halifax papers, advertising the sale of slaves. In 1764 the following appeared in the *Gazette*: "On Saturday next at 12 o'clock will be sold on the beach 2 hogshead of rum, 3 of sugar and 2 well grown negro girls, aged 14 and 12, to the highest bidder." I would venture an opinion that the sale on any beach in Nova Scotia today would call for some sharp bidding on the first packages mentioned and it is quite likely there would be a good attendance. Again the *Nova Scotia Gazette* and *Weekly Chronicle*, March 28th, 1775 — "a likely well made Negro boy about 16 years old was offered for sale." In January 1774 attention is called to an "able body wench about 21 years of age capable of performing both town and country work, and an exceedingly good cook." A girl like that would be worth her weight in gold today.

I have no doubt that masters were aggravated at times by the conduct of shiftless, idle, or mischievous servants, and now and again meted out what would seem to us today rather harsh treatment.

In the register of baptisms for the parish of St. Luke's there is frequent mention made from the year 1784 and after of Negro people, many no doubt slaves, as they are designated by one name only. I will mention a few of them: April, 1784, Sally, a black; same month, Abigail Mary; February, 1785, Peter, a black; May, 1786, Pomp, a black and Badus, a black, and a great many other entries of like nature. In the recording of baptisms I regret to say that a note appears now and again after certain names that leads one to believe that in those times there was a lack of regard for the marriage ceremony. It is related that two slaves, owned by Miss Polly Polhemus, a daughter of John Polhemus, one of the Loyalist captains at Annapolis Royal, arranged an exchange of partners. Miss Polhemus or any other outside party does not appear to have interfered with the compact and one of the worthy individuals continued to drive the carriage of his mistress from her residence near Clementsport to the parish church, a very picture of ebony dignity.

Quite a number of the Negro population of the days gone by of this vicinity are buried in the old military cemetery in this town. The southeast corner of the cemetery seems to have been allotted especially to them. There they lie under the shadow of the old willows, their graves for most part unmarked by any stone to identify their last resting place.

It is told of one of these old Negroes that he fell sick one day and he had, to see him, one of the two doctors who had practiced in the town at that time. After a few days, he felt that he was not making the improvement he should so he called in the other doctor. The other medical man looked his patient over and then said, "John, did Dr. so and so take your temperature when he was here?" "I don't know, doctor" was the feeble reply, "but I did miss my watch."

In 1801 at the September term of the Supreme Court, a very important case was tried in Nova Scotia; a slave named Jack ran away from James DeLancey near Round Hill and eventually found his way to Halifax and found employment on wages with Mr. Wm. Woodin. A demand was made by Thomas Ritchie, Esq., on behalf of Mr. DeLancey for the wages of the slave and later an action of trover was brought for the Negro by which Mr. DeLancey recovered a verdict for £70 damages. But the counsel for the defendant, R. J. Uniacke, moved the Court to arrest the judgment that an action of trover would not lie for conversion of a Negro in this province as here he could no more be the slave of Mr. DeLancey or any other person. At the September term of the Supreme Court in 1803 at Annapolis Royal, William Woodin was summoned to appear to answer to James DeLancey on the sum of £500 damages in a plea of trespass. The documents on file furnish no information as to the issue, but it is quite clear that Colonel DeLancey failed to regain possession of the notorious Jack.

A final effort for relief by legislative action was made by Nova Scotia Proprietors in 1808. During the session of that year, Mr. Warwick, member for the township of Digby, presented a petition from John Taylor and a number of other proprietors of Negro servants brought from the provinces, in which they stated that owing to the doubts entertained by the Courts, such property was being rendered useless, the Negro servants leaving their masters daily and setting them at defiance. In consequence of these facts, they prayed the passage for an act for "securing them their property or indemnifying them for their loss." It was no doubt with a view to such an end that Thos. Ritchie, member for Annapolis Royal, during the same session introduced a bill to regulate Negro servants within the province. This bill which passed its second reading in January 11th, 1808, but never became law, was in all probability the last struggle of a system which merited only death.

I recollect being in a stipendiary's court some years ago when a case for violation of what was popularly known as the Scott Act was being tried. The Counsel for the prosecution was a descendant of the Thos. Ritchie I have just mentioned, and is now one of the judges of the Supreme Court of this province. He was examining the star witness for the prosecution, or at any rate what he then supposed was the star witness, who was a coloured gentleman of some notoriety in this locality. The examination ran something like this — some of the names, of course, being changed. "Mr. Moses, you know Mr. Smith well?" "Yes indeed, sah, I know him well." "He keeps a store or place in the Town?" "Yes, sah." "Have you been in Mr. Smith's place within the last three months?" "Oh, yes, sah, in and out every day or so." "They tell me, Mr. Moses, that Mr. Smith keeps a little something in the way of liquor for sale." "Does he, now? Well, I'm mighty glad to know that, sah; when I want a little drop, I shall know where to go." All of which demonstrated the ability of the star witness to slip out from under.

And so we come down to the present day and when we look around us and see the present members of the Negro population of the county who are descendants of the different persons of the Negro race that we have had under discussion, one is bound to ask the reason why these people do not present a more prosperous appearance. It is a melancholy fact that notwithstanding all the present day advantages at their hands, the majority them are still "hewers of wood and drawers of water." It would appear that the great hardships their ancestors have gone through have left their stamp on the generations that followed and crushed out the desire to rise to better conditions.

It is pleasing to note, however, that there is one here and there who has achieved something above the common conditions of life of his fellows. Such cases merit, and usually receive, the approval and encouragement of the community with the hope that they will prove an example to others and stimulate them to attain the same or even better circumstances.

I am indebted to Mr. F. Watson Smith's valuable paper "The Slave in Canada" printed in the collection of the Nova Scotia Historical Society, Vol. X, for much help in the preparation of this paper.

For the stories contained in this booklet I am deeply grateful to a number of people who are no longer with us, also for the assistance of Miss Laura Hardy, museum assistant of Fort Anne Historical Museum.

— Charlotte Perkins

ABOUT THE AUTHOR

Charlotte Perkins was born in Annapolis Royal in 1878 and died in 1964. Known locally as Lottie, she worked tirelessly to document the prestigious past of her hometown, writing *The Romance of Old Annapolis Royal* which was published in 1924. A visual artist also, she drew the line drawings for the book.

The Writer